The Scandal of Redemption

The Scandal of Redemption

When God Liberates the Poor,
Saves Sinners, and Heals Nations

Oscar Romero

Edited by Carolyn Kurtz

Plough

Published by Plough Publishing House
Walden, New York
Robertsbridge, England
Elsmore, Australia
www.plough.com

Cover artwork copyright © Julie Lonneman. Photograph on page ii from Bettmann / Getty Images.

Diary entries from *Archbishop Oscar Romero: A Shepherd's Diary,* translated by Irene B. Hodgson (Cincinnati: St. Anthony Messenger Press, 1993). English translation copyright © 1993 by United States Conference of Catholic Bishops, Washington, DC. Used with permission. All rights reserved.

Homily excerpts from *A Prophetic Bishop Speaks to his People: The Complete Homilies of Archbishop Oscar Arnulfo Romero,* 6 vols., translated by Joseph Owens, SJ (Miami: Convivium Press, 2015, 2016). English translation copyright © 2015, 2016 by Convivium Press. Used with permission. All rights reserved.

A catalog record for this book is available from the British Library.
Library of Congress Cataloging-in-Publication Data

Names: Romero, ?Oscar A. (?Oscar Arnulfo), 1917-1980, author. | Kurtz, Carolyn, editor.
Title: The scandal of redemption : when God liberates the poor, saves sinners, and heals nations / Oscar Romero ; edited by Carolyn Kurtz.
Description: Walden : Plough Publishing House, 2018. | Includes bibliographical references.
Identifiers: LCCN 2017057265 (print) | LCCN 2018001476 (ebook) | ISBN 9780874861426 (epub) | ISBN 9780874861433 (mobi) | ISBN 9780874861440 (pdf) | ISBN 9780874861419 (pbk.)
Subjects: LCSH: Liberation theology. | Change--Religious aspects--Christianity.
Classification: LCC BX4705.R669 (ebook) | LCC BX4705.R669 A25 2018 (print) | DDC 282/.7284--dc23
LC record available at https://lccn.loc.gov/2017057265

Printed in the United States of America

Contents

Foreword

MY VIEW OF OSCAR ROMERO is shaped by my own
journey. When Romero was shot while celebrating
Mass on March 24, 1980, I was living in Lesotho, a
small mountainous kingdom completely surrounded
by the Republic of South Africa, having been banished
from South Africa for speaking out against injustice, as
Romero and many other religious leaders were doing at
the time. The South African state was enforcing apartheid, a form of constitutionalized racism. The United
Nations had declared that apartheid was a crime against
humanity, and the international Christian community
had said that it was heresy or false doctrine, yet the
apartheid state still claimed divine guidance and insisted
that it was a Christian state.

Like Romero, following Jesus was my desire from
early childhood. At the age of seventeen, I left New
Zealand and traveled to Australia to begin training for
the priesthood of the Anglican Church as well as to join
an Anglican religious order, the Society of the Sacred
Mission.

My religious order transferred me to South Africa in 1973. I imagined that when I arrived I would find three groups of people: the oppressed, the oppressors, and the third group to which I would belong: the human race. My first rude awakening was the realization that the color of my skin made me part of the oppressor group even if I did not wish to be. The day I arrived in South Africa I stopped being a human being and became a white man.

I was expelled from South Africa in September 1976. Just three months earlier, on June 16, 1976, the police and soldiers had begun shooting school children. This was a defining moment in my own life journey.

For Archbishop Romero, the turning point was the assassination of Father Rutilio Grande on March 12, 1977. As Romero said: "When I looked at Rutilio lying there dead I thought, 'If they have killed him for doing what he did, then I too have to walk the same path.'"

Unlike Archbishop Romero, I chose to join the political liberation movement. Like Romero, however, the only weapon I ever used was my tongue. For me, joining the liberation struggle was about recovering my own humanity, in solidarity with people of color struggling for their basic human rights. Soon after the blood of children poured out in the streets of South Africa, I was elected to be the national chaplain to Anglican students.

I began to speak out against the killing of children and the widespread detentions and torture.

The news of Romero's assassination certainly made me stop and consider what my actions might cost, and I'm sure people of faith engaged in similar struggles for justice around the globe could say the same. But more than that, his words and his witness gave us courage and determination to apply the words of Jesus even more clearly and boldly to the situations we faced. In 1982 there was a massacre in Maseru where forty-two people were shot dead by the South African Army. I was not there at the time but was believed by some of the church authorities to be one of the targets of the massacre. It was then that I made a vow that my own life would be dedicated to help end apartheid and build a society in which little children would go to bed safe and wake up safe.

Because I was on a hit list of the South African government, for several years I had to live in Zimbabwe, with armed police guards twenty-four hours a day. There, in April 1990, three months after Nelson Mandela was released from prison, I received in the post a letter bomb hidden inside the pages of two religious magazines. In the blast I lost both of my hands and an eye, and my eardrums were shattered.

When the bomb went off, I felt that God was with me in my crucifixion. I also felt that Mary, the mother of

Jesus, understood what I was experiencing. The prayers and love of people around the world were the vehicle that God used to make my bombing redemptive, to bring life out of death and good out of evil.

And once again, Romero's example spoke directly to me. I recalled his last words, moments before he was shot at the altar. "May this body that was immolated and this flesh that was sacrificed for humankind also nourish us so that we can give our bodies and our blood to suffering and to pain, as Christ did, not for our own sake but to bring justice and peace to our people."

I was particularly challenged and inspired by an interview Archbishop Romero gave just days before his death, in which he indicated that he wanted whoever would murder him to know that he forgave him. To this day, I don't know who sent me that bomb in April of 1990. But if that person is still a prisoner of what he did, I have a key and I would be happy to turn it.

My reflections on my own journey of healing, as well as on the journey of the people of South Africa, led me in time to establish the Institute for Healing of Memories. As part of the global work of this non-governmental organization, in November 2016 I was invited for the first time to visit the land of Oscar Romero, the only country named after the Savior of the world, to see if in some modest way we could contribute to the healing journey of the Salvadoran people. On All Saints Day 2016, at the Wall of Truth and Memory in San Salvador, I participated in an ecumenical memorial for the thousands disappeared and killed during the Salvadoran civil war. And I was able to kneel at the tomb of Oscar Romero, as well as at the spot where his assassination and martyrdom took place.

Tragically, the land of the Savior is still characterized by huge social violence and inequality. But Romero's witness lives on. As José Osvaldo Lopez, an Anglican in El Salvador, writes:

> With the life and works of Romero, I am certain that Jesus himself passed through El Salvador, leaving us a clear and strong message by his life example as a person and a pastor. Romero is for me not simply a pastoral model, but above all an enormous challenge, one that requires me as a Christian to assume a critical attitude against social and structural injustice. Yet Romero does not only challenge me to denounce injustice. Above all he invites me, calling on me forcefully, to love those around me. . . . By loving my brothers and sisters, I will not only be imitating Romero but also Jesus, with whom I will be contributing to building a better world. And in the end, I will be part of the construction of the true kingdom of God on earth.

As I seek to make my own humble contribution to the healing of the human family, I continue to be inspired by the life and legacy of Oscar Romero. It is my hope and prayer that through this book he will do the same for another generation of people who hunger and thirst for righteousness. I have no doubt that if you read this book with an open heart, it will deepen your own faith and commitment to work for justice and to participate in God's dream for all of us.

Father Michael Lapsley, SSM
Director, Institute for Healing of Memories
South Africa

Who Was Oscar Romero?

OSCAR ROMERO spent just three years as Archbishop of San Salvador, but by the time he was murdered in 1980 he had become a shepherd to the people of El Salvador and the outspoken advocate of its oppressed peasants. In those three years, he built an inspiring and challenging legacy for all those who seek to follow Christ today.

Romero's deep faith in God and his love for and trust in the church as a people committed to Christ still ring through his homilies. These weekly sermons preserve the record of atrocities committed against his people during the beginning of the Civil War in El Salvador; more importantly, they record Romero's response to the violence in his country. Over and over, he challenged those in power to care for their countrymen; he encouraged the campesinos to pray, to counter hatred with love; he pleaded with the people to live more truly by the vision of the New Testament; and he reminded his entire audience of how Jesus came to earth in poverty, enduring the pain and humiliation of the cross before the triumph of his resurrection. Because Christ knows all the suffering on earth, Romero says, we can believe in and work for his kingdom on earth.

BORN IN 1917, Romero was no child of privilege. With his five brothers and sisters, he slept on the floor of the small family home. The local school only offered three years of education, and though he displayed an aptitude for learning, his father began to train him as a carpenter. But when Romero was thirteen, he told his parents he wanted to study for the priesthood. He entered seminary when he was fourteen, completing his studies in Rome. In 1942, at the age of twenty-five, he was ordained as a priest, and from 1943 to 1967 he served as pastor of the cathedral parish of San Miguel, El Salvador.

It was, in many ways, a conventional story. But the times were not conventional. In 1962, Pope John XXIII convened the Second Vatican Council to address the relationship of the Roman Catholic Church to the modern world. The council closed three years later, having enacted sweeping reforms. The council emphasized that the church is God's people, not a human institution, and that it is God's means to serve the world by bringing Christ's salvation into it.

Three years later, in 1968, the bishops of Latin America met at Medellín, Colombia, to consider how the reforms of Vatican II should be applied to their own countries. The church, affirmed the bishops, must serve society. To do so, it must understand how power is used and abused – how people are subject to systematic economic and political exploitation. And the church must bring the gospel of Jesus into these concrete realities. This Gospel is not only a message of personal salvation from sin and entrance into the eternal kingdom of God, but also the transformation of injustice in the present. The kingdom, the bishops believed, could come on earth as it is in heaven, and it was part of the proper work of the church to help bring it to reality.

Three hundred million people under these bishops' care in Latin America were living in poverty and experiencing the daily injustice of political oppression. Therefore, shepherding these people must include not just exhorting them to holiness and extending Christ's offer of forgiveness, but also improving their circumstances. The extreme poverty of many in a society where a few lived in luxury was a situation that cried out for redress. And so the church must cry out too, taking what came to be called the "preferential option for the poor."

"Peace is not found," wrote the Medellín bishops, "it is built. The Christian is the artisan of peace. This task . . . has a special character in our continent; thus, the people of God in Latin America, following the example of

Christ, must resist personal and collective injustice with unselfish courage and fearlessness."

This recognition became the seed of liberation theology. Romero never aligned himself explicitly with the movement, but he embraced many of its radical critiques of the existing order, and certainly believed that the gospel called him to speak up for the least powerful.

While some liberation theologians defended the use of armed force in their efforts to achieve structural change, Romero did not. He simply told the truth about what following Jesus would look like for the ruling class of El Salvador, and for the people. This was a radical message. The bishops were saying that the call of the gospel would not let them leave unjust social arrangements alone: that love for both the poor and the oligarchs demanded change. In El Salvador, and elsewhere in Latin America, many church leaders had allied themselves with the upper class. But by the 1970s, some parish priests had begun to emphasize social justice and economic reform, reflecting Christ's concern for the poor and his call to share wealth. Some priests were also encouraging the formation of "base ecclesial communities" in which believers gathered to read and discuss Christian teaching on their own. Priests were often only irregularly available, so these communities provided spiritual encouragement for the peasants.

The teaching discussed in these base communities often focused on the church's social doctrine, and peasants began to talk boldly about the injustice they saw in their society. Many landowners feared these new groups, denouncing them as communist. Tensions grew as the priests carried out the recommendations of Vatican II and Medellín, giving the government excuse to expel foreign priests, who they claimed were stirring up trouble.

THROUGHOUT THIS STORMY HISTORY, Oscar Romero had been at work. During his time as pastor of San Miguel, his parishioners had appreciated his lively preaching and the many parish activities he organized. When, in 1966, he took over as editor of the archdiocesan newspaper, they read what he had to say. But he was by no means one of the radical priests who were making so much trouble. Ordained a bishop in 1970, he was assigned to San Salvador, the capital city. Many churchmen there, including the elderly Archbishop Luis Chávez y González, had embraced the radical message of the Medellín meeting. Bishop Romero was not part of this contingent. Though increasingly troubled by what he saw, he was still attempting to walk a line. When the police massacred five peasants in his district, he protested strongly in a letter to the president but kept his public comments to a minimum.

When the time came for a new archbishop to be appointed, those who backed Romero were the elites of San Salvador. They considered him "safe." With their support, in 1977 Romero was appointed by the Vatican to be Archbishop of San Salvador – effectively responsible for shepherding the Catholic Church in all of El Salvador.

The installation of the new archbishop was not the only change in leadership going on in El Salvador that February. A presidential election had been held two days before Romero took up his new role. Thanks to massive voter fraud, including assaults and intimidation at the polls, the government party candidate, a darling of the oligarchs, was named the winner. A massive crowd, as many as sixty thousand people, flocked to the city's central square – to celebrate Mass, and to protest the election results: one purpose bled into the other. After the Mass, the police called for the gathered people to disperse. Most did – but the police opened fire on the two thousand or so who remained. The protesters ran to seek sanctuary in San Rosario, the church that bordered the square, and were besieged until the former archbishop, Chávez y González, arranged a truce.

Protests continued and two days later troops once again fired on the crowd in the square. Somewhere between forty and three hundred people were killed.

The violence was not confined to the city: the National Guard had arrested and tortured a parish priest in a rural district who was considered one of the troublemakers; other priests were being expelled.

THEN, THREE WEEKS after Romero's appointment, one of those troublesome priests, Rutilio Grande, was shot down by gunmen. Everyone suspected that the government and the clique of oligarchs were responsible: Father Grande had been one of the most outspoken of those who were critical of the regime, defending the peasants, and had been active in helping to organize base communities. He had also been Archbishop Romero's dear friend.

Romero traveled to the rural church where Grande's body had been taken, and spent that day praying and listening to stories of violence and exploitation from the peasants whom Grande had served, and stories of his care for them. At the homily for the funeral Mass, Romero called Grande's death what it was: an assassination. He said what everyone knew: Father Grande had been killed precisely for speaking up on behalf of the peasants.

"We have asked the legal authorities to shed light on this criminal act," Romero said, "for they have in their hands the instruments of this nation's justice and they must clarify this situation. We are not accusing anyone nor are we making judgments before we have all the facts. We hope to hear the voice of an impartial justice since the cause of love cannot be separated from justice. There can be no true peace or love that is based on injustice or violence or intrigue."

His meaning was unmistakable. It was the violence and intrigue in the government-supported military itself that he had in his sights. But even in this, he refused to compromise the gospel:

> Who knows if those responsible for this criminal act and who have been excommunicated are listening to the radio in their hideout and hearing these words? My dear criminals, we want to tell you that we love you and we ask God to pour forth repentance into your hearts.

Romero returned to San Salvador, where he met with the bishops and priests who served under him. And then he acted. He closed all the country's Catholic schools for three days of mourning. The following Sunday, he had every priest in El Salvador refrain from saying Mass. Instead, he held a single Mass outside San Salvador Cathedral. The crowds were larger even than those at the Mass and protest two weeks earlier. Romero showed his people that he would not be distancing himself from the kind of work that Grande had been doing. Grande had, he said, given his life in the proclamation of the gospel, and Romero publicly thanked the other priests who were doing the same kind of work. After the homily, he demanded that the government investigate the events surrounding the assassination of Grande, saying that he would not participate in any formal governmental event until the assassins had been brought to justice.

ROMERO HAD DECLARED HIMSELF. And from that moment, he would not back down, and he would not be quiet. For the following three years, in his homilies – which were broadcast over the radio – and in the archdiocesan newspaper, Archbishop Romero spoke to the people, to the oligarchs, and to the government, and he spoke truth.

His homilies called his listeners to Christ's message of love and radical forgiveness, and to the need for justice. He called those in power to take care lest they violate that justice. He called all to Christ, teaching the message of the gospel and the hope of eternal life in Christ's kingdom even as he also taught the campesinos who listened to him that the love and justice of this kingdom was something that they could and should hope for, pray for, and work for now, in El Salvador, in their lives. He warned them away from the guerrilla warfare to which some, in desperation, were turning; the way of Christ pointed to a better response. But this response was not passivity or acquiescence:

We have never preached violence, except the violence of the love that led Christ to be nailed to a cross. We preach only the violence that we must each do to ourselves to overcome selfishness and to eliminate the cruel inequalities among us. This is not the violence of the sword, the violence of hatred. It is the violence of love and fraternity, the violence that chooses to beat weapons into sickles for work.

All conversion, all change, began with the heart; with God drawing people to him to shape them into a community of love. And this community could and must include those who had formerly been enemies; Romero extended Christ's forgiveness to the government's killers as well.

There is no justice without truth. Murders of peasants and attacks on priests were common in El Salvador, and would become more so in the years to follow. But they were under-reported, the news often distorted. The press was in the pocket of the wealthy. The Jesuit seminary had been bombed six times the previous year, and opposition leaders and those who spoke up were regularly "disappeared," but El Salvador's newspapers were reluctant to investigate these government crimes.

Each of Archbishop Romero's homilies included a summary of the events of the week: he gathered reports of as many of the disappearances, murders, and attacks as he could, quoting eyewitness testimony and pointing out the frequent falsity of the official version of events as reported by the compromised news media. He was not reckless in accusation, but he also did not hesitate to use his homilies to present evidence showing the complicity of the national security forces in various assassinations. He spoke these homilies to an audience that eventually included half of El Salvador's city-dwellers and three quarters of the campesinos – except when the Salvadoran military succeeded in jamming the signal that came out of the cathedral in downtown San Salvador. Twice, the radio station was damaged by bombs; twice, Romero rebuilt it. His listeners included peasants in distant villages and urban workers, members of the government and of the army, anti-government guerilas in their camps and not a few of the oligarchs themselves, in their living rooms in San Salvador.

Never for a moment, however, did Romero lose track of the central purpose of these homilies: not to report the news of the day but to proclaim the gospel. "I want to reaffirm that my sermons are not political," he said. "Naturally, they touch on politics, and they touch on the reality of the people, but their aim is to shed light and to tell you what it is that God wants."

During the three years of Romero's leadership, pres-sures only increased. There were moments of hope – a military coup installed a new government, and he continued to try to work with the country's political leaders, who sought both his support and his silence. He offered his support in whatever he felt was beneficial for the people, but was never silent in the face of ongoing repression. During this time, Romero also faced a growing rift in the church hierarchy: many opposed him, believing that he was only stirring up trouble, afraid of repercussions. Particularly hard was the opposition of all but one of his fellow bishops: this lack of unity, he saw, contributed to the escalating repression and violence inflicted on the suffering people.

He met with leaders of the leftist revolutionary groups who periodically occupied church buildings. He offered the hospitality of the church to those who needed sanctuary from the vengeance of the military, but refused to condone the violence or the kidnappings that were the tactics of the guerilla groups. For his willingness to speak with members of these groups, and for his condemnation of the violence of the military, he was called a communist, accused of abandoning or politicizing the gospel.

In spite of this severe opposition, Romero sought every week to lead his flock to faith, hope, and love through following Christ. He sensed that his time was short. In the years he served as archbishop, dozens of priests who spoke out against the violence of the regime and the economic inequalities of the country were imprisoned, tortured, or expelled. Five were murdered. He realized that in all probability, his own turn was coming. In late February of 1980, he wrote:

I express my consecration to the heart of Jesus. . . . I place under his loving providence all my life, and I accept with faith in him my death, however hard it be. . . . For me to be happy and confident, it is sufficient to know with assurance that in him is my life and my death, that in spite of my sins I have placed my trust in him and shall not be disappointed, and others will carry on with greater wisdom and holiness the works of the church and the nation.

Several days later, in an interview, he told the reporter, "You can tell them, if they succeed in killing me, then I pardon them, and I bless those who may carry out the killing. But I wish that they could realize that they are wasting their time. A bishop will die, but the church of God – the people – will never perish."

On March 23, in his homily, he spoke directly to the army:

Brothers, you are a part of our own people. You are killing your own brother and sister campesinos, and against any order a man may give to kill, God's law must prevail: "You shall not kill!" (Exod. 20:13). No soldier is obliged to obey an order against the law of God. No one has to observe an immoral law. It is time now for you to reclaim your conscience and obey your conscience rather than the command to sin. . . . In the name of God, then, and in the name of this suffering people whose laments rise up each day more tumultuously toward heaven, I beg you, I beseech you, I order you in the name of God: stop the repression!

Archbishop Oscar Romero was shot to death the next day, on March 24, 1980, as he held a memorial Mass for a friend's mother.

ROMERO'S ASSASSINATION was only one of an estimated seventy-five thousand deaths during what became a full-fledged civil war in El Salvador. But through his death his witness has only grown. Romero was entrusted with teaching and leading Christ's flock in a particular place and time, and that is what he did. He followed his Lord. He called wrong wrong. He spoke on behalf of the poor, called for faith in God, and enjoined all to obey Christ's teachings. He pointed men and women of every position towards the hope of the gospel and pleaded for unity among believers.

The selections in this book come from Romero's radio homilies and from the diary he kept for the last several years of his life (1977–1980). Originally addressed to his own people, to inspire and encourage them as they sought God's kingdom in the midst of unimaginable hardship, his words now speak across time and across all historical and cultural contexts to anyone who seeks God's justice and redemption today. Romero's signal, despite all opposition, has gotten through.

Carolyn Kurtz

Saturday, April 8

A visit to the town of Dulce Nombre de María in
the department of Chalatenango, arranged with the
Oblate Sisters of the Sacred Heart, who work in that
city and have some problems locally. Nevertheless,
my arrival there and my visit were very moving
experiences for me: the meeting in the town, the
celebration of Mass, the meeting we had later with the
celebrants of the word, catechists, and other groups
active in the church. It is a community that gives real
hope, a community that is alive. . . .

A disagreeable detail when I entered the town was
the aggressive posture of a member of the National
Guard, who only got out of the middle of the street
when the crowd that accompanied me at that time was
very near. I noticed how surprised people, especially
the children, were by this gesture, and I could easily
see that they are planting seeds in Dulce Nombre de
María of what they call "a psychological war." I saw

this in the people who arrived from the small villages —
a kind of fear, worse because they had circulated
a rumor that I was going to come with some guerillas
and they tried to dissuade the people from going to
participate in the ceremony and the meetings that we
had planned.

I

The Creator

HOW WONDERFUL IT IS, sisters and brothers, to feel
governed by God, placed under God's sovereignty! That
is what the Holy Bible means when it says that there is no
power that does not come from God and that authority
must be obeyed because it comes from God (Rom. 13:1).
But the Bible also says that the human sovereign, the
one who commands, must not command anything apart
from what God wants; moreover, it says that authority
is to be respected only because it reflects God's sacred
power. When human authority contravenes God's law
and violates the rights, the freedom, and the dignity of
human beings, then it is time to cry out as Saint Peter
did in the Bible, "We must obey God rather than men"
(Acts 5:29). All power comes from God, and therefore
rulers cannot use their authority capriciously but only
according to the Lord's will. God's providence aims to
govern the nations, and the rulers are only his ministers,
servants of God like all the rest of his creatures.

THE BIBLE SAYS that he is a just God (Wis. 12:13–18): "You do not judge unjustly." "Your power is the source of justice." Consider the richness of this concept of justice. Justice is the manifestation of power. A power is not true power unless it is just. God himself, who can do what he wills, does not abuse power; indeed, he cannot abuse it because he is just; he is justice par excellence. God's power is illuminated by his infinite justice. "You judge with moderation." This is the eternal serenity of God; he does not get impatient. He is the God who holds the reins of all peoples and all human beings, and that is why his justice is restrained; it is justice that is serene and holy.

Still another title that comes from today's readings is "merciful God." "Your universal sovereignty makes you spare all." "You govern us with great indulgence because you can do whatever you want."... Dear sisters and brothers, this is our God. Let us not forget him; let us respect him, realizing that he is the source of all the joy and the confidence of our faith. May the God that Jesus Christ reveals to us as Father, as providence, as goodness, always capture our hearts so that we will serve him not out of fear but out of love.

ONLY WHEN WE SEE the God of our Lord Jesus Christ illuminating our dawns, our seas, and our volcanoes will we understand that God has created a world out of love to give it to his children, with whom he wants to enter into the communion of family. In this way we understand how the earth groans beneath the weight of sin (Rom. 8:22) because humanity has not understood that the whole of creation exists for the happiness of all human beings and not for us to be comfortably settled here on earth.

THERE IS NO ANONYMOUS PERSON among those of us who are here. All of you have your own individual histories, even the humblest of persons, even the smallest child who has come to this Mass, even the poorest and sickest folks listening by radio, all those people about whom nobody will talk in the history books. God has loved each of you singularly, as an unrepeatable phenomenon. God has not made human beings in a mold. . . . It was not my parents who gave me being; they were simply instruments or means that God used to give me life. . . . Even prior to the months of my gestation, I existed in the mind of God as a project which, if brought to fulfillment, would make of me a saint because a saint is nothing else than the full realization of a life according to the design of God.

THE WHOLE HISTORY OF ISRAEL is the story of humanity's return to God after breaking away. The whole marvelous book of Exodus tells how the people left slavery in Egypt and journeyed toward the Promised Land; it is a symbol of pilgrimage, of return, of the search for reconciliation. . . . The people had no certainty about the future; they lived believing in the land God had promised them, though they didn't know where it was. They seemed crazy but they weren't crazy; they were people of faith: "God has promised it! He will make it happen!" . . .

There is a wonderful relationship here with our own situation in El Salvador, where the land is being fought over. Let us not forget that the land is closely tied to the blessings and promises of God. . . . Not having land is a consequence of sin. When Adam left paradise, he was a man without land as the result of sin. Now Israel, pardoned by God, has returned to the land and can eat of the fruits and the grains of the earth. God gives his blessings in the form of land. The land contains much of God, and therefore it groans when the unjust monopolize it and leave no space for others. Agrarian reform is a theological necessity. A country's land cannot remain in the hands of just a few; it must be given to all so that all can share in the blessings God gives through the land. . . . There will be no true reconciliation between our people and God as long as there is no just distribution, as long as the goods of our Salvadoran land do not bring benefits and happiness to all Salvadorans.

LET US LOOK THIS MORNING, sisters and brothers, on this church which extends far beyond the tiny geographical speck which is El Salvador. We feel that we are sisters and brothers with all the peoples of Central America, of this continent of North America, of Canada, of Europe. And we are all called to follow this light.

What is marvelous to consider is that in this convocation of peoples God – the God of nations – respects the freedom, the customs, and the unique way of being of each people. The reading from Isaiah tells us, "The riches of the sea shall be emptied before you, and the wealth of nations shall be brought to you" (Isa. 60:5). This kingdom of God certainly has no need of our material goods, but we recognize that God is the origin of our coffee crops, our sugar cane, our cotton fields, all our wealth, and all the wealth of the world, and he has a right to all of these things. So we generously offer these things to God, recognizing that he owns them all, just as the magi placed gold, frankincense, and myrrh by the Christ Child's crib. Everything that the world produces is God's. The true wealth of the church as God's kingdom is the realization that all the differences among the world's peoples come from God. God has created in this world a kingdom rich like no other because all the marvels of the earth are his. Everything produced by human cultures belongs to God. It is God who promotes and guides all the wealth and progress of the peoples.

Under the sign of bread and wine the priests of all latitudes of the world tell the Lord that we are offering him, in this bread and in this wine, the work of human hands. When we say "the work of human hands," we understand this to be the work of all the latitudes of the world. We offer it all to God because without God human labors and human progress have no meaning. We all contribute to this kingdom of God.

Monday, October 9

In the afternoon I went to celebrate Mass in the village of La Loma in the territory of San Pedro Perulapán, a Mass offered for two murdered peasants who were found near the Apulo Highway. I was surprised by the size of the crowd waiting for me. I addressed words of comfort to them. The mothers, wives, children, and other family members and friends of those murdered were present there.

All of them reflected the fear being sowed in these sectors of our dear people — fear that is justified by the repression and abuse of authority by the security forces and, especially, by the armed peasant groups like the organization ORDEN. In fact, while we celebrated Mass, they appeared with their curved knives, some of them unsheathed, and they stood where they could watch the crowd. They wrote down the license number of the van in which we had come with the sisters. And there was an aggressive attitude, or, at least, a mistrustful wariness. I understood the peasants' fears, why many men sleep somewhere other than at their homes for fear of being taken by surprise at night.

2

The Word Made Flesh

CHRIST IS BEING BORN FOR US today. That is what the prophet Isaiah has told us: "A child has been born to us; a child has been given to us" (Isa. 9:6). He is here now for us.

Let us truly experience it this way, because I know that each one of you feels the need, just as I do, to embrace as our very own child that Jesus who is born for all and who, in giving himself to all, gives himself to me in particular. Indeed, each of us can speak in the first person as does Saint Paul: "He loved me, and he handed himself over for me" (Gal. 2:20). Let each of us truly proclaim, "The Lord is the redeemer of my family; he is my companion in life, my confidant in time of anguish, my own redeemer who is at the same time the redeemer of all."

"GOD SO LOVED THE WORLD that he gave his only Son, so that everyone who believes in him might not perish but might have eternal life" (John 3:16). That is the reason for the coming of the messenger of eternal life, the only Son of God, the One who in his divine essence has received the quality of Word, of Son. He is the whole eternal nature of God, the whole of life without end, the light that disperses all shadows, the solution of all problems, the love of all who despair, the joy of all who are sad. Whoever possesses this Son of God lacks for nothing.

IF WE WANT TO FIND the child Jesus today, we shouldn't contemplate the lovely figures in our nativity scenes. We should look for him among the malnourished children who went to bed tonight without anything to eat. We should look for him among the poor newspaper boys who will sleep tonight on doorsteps, wrapped in their papers. . . . In taking all this upon himself, the God of the poor is showing us the redemptive value of human suffering. He is showing us the value it has for redeeming the poverty and suffering which are the world's cross.

There is no redemption without the cross, but that does not mean our poor people should be passive. We were indoctrinating the poor when we told them, "It is God's will for you to live poor and hopeless on the margins of society." That is not true! God in no way wants social injustice. . . . The greatest violence comes from those who deprive so many people of happiness, from those who are killing the many people who are starving. God is telling the poor, as he told the oppressed Christ when he was carrying his cross, "You will save the world by making your suffering a protest of salvation and by not conforming to what God does not want. You will save the world if you die in your poverty while yearning for better times, making your whole life a prayer, and embodying everything that seeks to liberate the people from this situation."

MARY KNEW HOW TO ENDURE flight into exile, marginalization, poverty, oppression. Mary was the daughter of a people dominated by the Roman Empire. She saw her son taken prisoner and tortured. She saw him die unjustly on the cross. Mary cries out in holy defiance, declaring that God "will send the proud and the arrogant away empty-handed and, if necessary, bring the mighty down from their thrones. At the same time he will give his grace to the lowly, to those who trust in his mercy" (Luke 1:52–53).

By being born this way, Christ has a lesson for the poor countries and the humble hostels; he has a lesson for those freezing at night in the coffee harvest and those sweating by day in the cotton fields. He is teaching them that all this signifies something and that we shouldn't miss the meaning of suffering. Dear brothers and sisters, if there is one thing that makes me sad in this hour of El Salvador's redemption, it is the thought that many false redeemers are allowing the suffering that is our people's force of redemption to go to waste. They use the people's hunger and marginalization for demagoguery. The people's suffering should not be made a motive for resentment and desperation; it should make people look to the justice of God and realize that this situation must change. And if necessary, like those who have already given their lives, we must be ready to die, but always with the hope that comes from our Christian faith.

How I wish that child, nestled in straw and humble cloth, would speak to us this Christmas of the sublime value of poverty! How I wish that all of us who are reflecting here would bestow divine value on our sufferings great and small! Starting tonight, let us be more intent on offering to God whatever we suffer.

SAINT PAUL TOLD THE CORINTHIANS, "Our message to you is not yes and no. We announce Christ, who is the eternal yes of God" (2 Cor. 1:18–19). What a beautiful name for Christ: the yes of God's promises! Christ is the yes in whom God has promised such extraordinary marvels as a new salvation, forgiveness of sins, and a call to all nations to form one single people united in love. God does not repent of his promises but fulfills them in Christ, even when that Son of his heart is taken and nailed on a cross. If that is the necessary condition for the fulfillment of God's promises, Christ is willing to die crucified. The sacrifice is the seal on God's great promises, and that's why Saint Paul says that those who try to be faithful to God say amen to him (2 Cor. 1:20). This morning let us reassess that timeworn word, amen. Perhaps we use it so much it has lost its meaning for us, for in the liturgy when we say amen, we are really making an act of faith. The most beautiful word we can say is yes, for it is our human yes to God through Christ.

Christ is humanity's amen to God. In Christ the hopes of all nations and of every person become amen because in Christ the promises of God become yes. In Christ is found the zone where those who are most needy and hopeless – the sinful people, the benighted societies – can glimpse the hope offered by a God who still loves us. That statement of Saint Paul, "Christ continues to be the yes" is a Greek grammatical construction, a tense that doesn't exist in our Spanish language. It means that what happened then continues to be a reality down through the centuries: Christ is alive, and he lives in his church, and he lives in Latin America.

AS WE BEHOLD THE RISEN CHRIST, our faith should overflow with gratitude and delight and hope. We should tell him, "You are the God who became man and

who for love of humankind was not afraid to hide your
grandeur as God and pass through this world as a man
like any other. So little did you distinguish yourself from
others that they associated you with criminals, and you
died as an outlaw on the cross on Calvary. They buried
you in the garbage dump of those who were crucified,
but from there, from the garbage dump, from the depths
of the abyss, from the descent into the realms of shadow
and death, you now rise up as the divine risen One, truly
anointed by God with the power of the Holy Spirit"
(Acts 10:38).

This is where the incarnation of Christ is crowned.
That God-Child whom the Virgin held in her arms, that
child she caressed and nursed at her breasts, that man his
enemies felt free to beat and despise – he was the flesh
of God. God was there. God was embodied in Christ.
The glory of the resurrection was necessary so that we
humans could come to understand that the dignity of
God is found in Christ humiliated and crucified, in
Christ who for us is God made a man who understands
us, in Christ who felt human exhaustion and sweat and
anguish. Now we see it when the glory of God pours
forth from his every pore, when his whole appearance
and his whole being seem more like the bright sun than
some mortal creature. Now we understand what Saint
Paul assures us about the resurrection: "What was sown
in ignominy is reaped in glory; what was sown in a

mortal tomb and seen as death is reaped in glorious and immortal resurrection and will never die again" (1 Cor. 15:42–44). Death will have no dominion over him. He is eternal youth, eternal beauty, eternal springtime; he is life without illness or decline but only the fullness of joy and happiness.

HE IS MESSIAH AND LORD, *Kyrios*, emperor and king, not with vain and grandiose triumphalism but with a divine royalty that makes him all-powerful, that makes him present in his church, that makes him the architect of history, that makes him the cornerstone of all human movements, and that makes him the compass that guides all of history toward its true destiny. He is the Lord of history, the Lord of ages, the Lord of eternity. He is the key which encompasses past, present, and future. "Christ forever," says Saint Paul. Christ is the Lord. Christ lives. Christ has risen, and death no longer has dominion over him. But this Christ presents himself as the Good Shepherd. What a marvelous thing, to consider that this powerful king, this man who bears the marks of all his suffering now made into glorious stars, is now our great liberator and our great shepherd!

THE PROPHECY OF ISAIAH tells us that the Servant of Yahweh will conquer and subject all the nations of the world, but he is not someone who will go shouting angrily through the streets. He is not unfeeling and violent but, rather, gentle and humble. Listen to what Isaiah says about this Servant: "A bruised reed he shall not break and a smoldering wick he shall not quench" (Isa. 42:3). What a magnificent image to describe the mercy of this redemption that is being offered to those who experience despair and to a people that feels like a candle that's about to be extinguished. Even if we feel profound frustration because of our own sins, the sins of the social classes, or the political abuses – even if we feel like a nation unworthy of the name, a people that does not deserve the mercy of God, this prophecy should still fill us with hope: "A bruised reed he shall not break, and a wick that still has a flickering of flame he shall not quench." In El Salvador we still have the ability to remake ourselves. The lamp of our faith and our hope can still be rekindled because our hope is here, in the Servant of Yahweh, Christ, who comes to free us from every form of slavery. He is our hope.

AS LONG AS WE DO NOT SEE Christ as true God and true man, we cannot understand the church or the saving mystery of the Lord. That is why God became man: so that by means of this God-man we might enter into the mystery of the divine. "I am the way. No one comes to the Father except through me" (John 14:6). God did not come to save humankind except through Jesus Christ, the only mediator. Blessed are those who know and believe in Jesus! Blessed are those who are aware, even in the midst of these dark hours of our history, that Christ lives! He lives powerfully as God, and he lives caringly as man. He is a man of our ways; he is a man of our history; he is a man like the one in a popular hymn. "God appears as a worker, as one walking in the park, working on the highway, or repairing tires in a gas station. God is incarnate in every person and understands everyone who wants to follow him and love him."* That is why Jesus said, "Whatever you do for one of these, you do it for me" (Matt. 25:40). He is the way to know humanity, just as he is the way to know God. No one can come to God except across this bridge, this way that is our Lord Jesus Christ. . . .

This Christ comes, and he proclaims, "Whoever believes in me will do the works that I do and will do greater ones than these" (John 14:12). What does this mean? It means that all the saving power that Jesus brought from God will now be entrusted to this group that forms the newborn church, so that over the centuries and among many peoples the church will do greater things than Christ in a geographical and numerical

---

* A reference to the entrance hymn of the *Misa campesina nicaragüense,* by Carlos Mejía Godoy.

sense. He saved the world with an objective redemption, we might say, by dying on the cross and leaving us the fountain of redemption. But his disciples have to set up channels to distribute this saving work to the whole world. Christ could already see his church extended among all peoples and doing greater things than he was able to do personally.

CHRISTIANS MUST ALWAYS NOURISH in their hearts the fullness of joy. Try to do that, sisters and brothers. I have tried it many times, and in the most bitter situations, when slander and persecution are at their worst, I have united myself intimately with Christ as my friend, and I have tasted a sweetness that all the joys of earth cannot give. It is the joy of God's intimacy, the profoundest joy the heart can experience, even when people don't understand you. Christ pronounced these words of joy on the tragic last night of his life, knowing that the next day even his disciples would abandon him. No doubt there was fullness of joy in the depths of Christ's soul even when he was ascending Calvary in the bitter agony of his passion, because he was doing the will of his Father and he felt that God was not abandoning him despite all appearances of abandonment. "I have told you this so that my joy may be in you and your joy may be complete" (John 15:11).

Sunday, April 2

In the evening, at six-thirty, in Colonia Miramonte, in the parish Church of the Resurrection . . . the parish community came in great numbers, filling the church. . . . I preached on the Gospel and made reference to the empty tomb of the risen Jesus and to the sealed tomb of Father Alfonso Navarro,* who just last year, in this very celebration, had showed such a pastor's enthusiasm in a parish that bears witness to the resurrection of Christ. His tomb was sealed after he was murdered, one of two priests shot dead this last year. His sealed tomb could be perceived as a failure of the redemption and resurrection of Christ and yet it is a sign of hope. Our dead will be raised and the tombs of our dead that today are sealed by the triumph of death will one day also be like that of Christ — empty tombs. Christ's empty tomb is a sign of the final victory, of redemption realized. Until then, we must struggle, we must work so that the message of

---

* Shot in his rectory on May 11, 1977, along with a 14-year-old boy

that empty tomb of Christ may enlighten all our work
on earth with hope until the fulfillment of the Lord's
redemption.

3

Redemption

CHRIST INCARNATES THE WHOLE HISTORY
of salvation. He had told the Samaritan woman, "The
hour is coming when you will worship the Father
neither on this mountain nor in Jerusalem, for God
seeks worshipers in spirit and in truth" (John 4:23). On
this night, the night before his execution, one of the
most serious accusations against Christ was repeated
before the Sanhedrin. He had said he would destroy the
temple and in three days rebuild it (Matt. 26:61). The
Gospel makes it clear that the temple to be destroyed
was his body because his body was the temple where the
covenant, God's victory, and the liberation of the people
of Israel would take place (John 2:21). He was temple,
victim, priest, and altar. He is the totality of redemption.

In Christ, our Lord, becomes incarnate all the gratitude of the people of Israel to the God who freed them.
In Christ, our Lord, becomes incarnate all the patriotic
hope of Israel and all the hopes of humankind. This
night Christ, our Lord, senses that he is "the lamb who

takes away the sins of the world" (John 1:29) and that his is the blood that will seal with freedom the hearts of all who truly want to be free. From this night on he is the priest who lifts adoration to the Father and brings from the Father forgiveness and blessings for his people.

Tomorrow, Good Friday, the torment of Christ culminates with his crucifixion, but from this evening on, the memorial of that passion remains here with us. Christ dying on the cross is the Lamb whose blood marks the hearts of those who believe in him; they will be free and will not suffer the torments of sin. He is the one who comes to take away the sin of the world, the one who comes to fill our hearts with hope. Sisters and brothers, blessed are Christians this night as we celebrate the Lord's Supper in this cathedral, and also in the parish churches, in the chapels, and in the communities throughout the archdiocese. Today we form part of the Israelite family that slaughters the Lamb who is Christ himself and that eats his flesh, which is our communion: "Take and eat, for this is my body that is given for you. Take and drink, for this is the cup of my blood, which will be shed for you for the forgiveness of sins" (Luke 22:19–20).

"THE SERVANT OF GOD IS LIKE a lamb led to the slaughter; he bore the iniquities of all people! We saw him, and his appearance was beyond that of mortals. He was so horrifying that people turned away from him in disgust and in fear. He was killed as no one had ever been killed before. He was tortured beyond limits and humiliated to the depths" (Isa. 53:2–4, 7). Inspired by God, the prophet Isaiah anticipated by seven centuries what is happening this afternoon: the humiliation of the Lamb.

These are unparalleled words. That is why I said that instead of talking we need to love, to meditate, to behold – with repugnance if need be – what has remained of Christ's appearance. He has become like a worm that squirms in the dust of the earth, amid saliva and blood, afflicted with incredible pain, truly made an outcast of humanity. It can hardly be described. This Good Friday each one of us needs to contemplate that victim with the eyes of the soul and consider how our sins have left him. For Christ does not suffer for his own faults; Christ made himself responsible for the sins of all of us. If you want to measure the gravity of your sins, simply look at Christ crucified and say in all honesty, "I have left him like this. I killed him. To cleanse me of my filth he became filth. To cleanse me of my abominations he became abominable." The word seems almost blasphemous, but it is spoken by the sacred scriptures: "The one who had no sin became for our sake sin; he was cursed and punished by God (2 Cor. 5:21; Gal. 3:13). This is Christ, the lightning rod of humanity. On him were discharged all the lightning bolts of divine anger to free us who were the ones who should have been struck down because we caused the curse each time we sinned.

YES, IN CHRIST IS REVEALED the mystery of love, how God has loved us, as the apostle writes: "God so loved the world that he gave his only Son" (John 3:16). What father hands over his son so that a prisoner or slave might be saved? That is what the eternal Father has done; he gave us his Son, his Word, his life, and in Christ we can recover God's life. Sins are forgiven because Christ became the price for our debt, and now we can all die with the hope of heaven because Christ has offered to open for us the gates of heaven even though we are sinners. We need only repent and be converted and return to him who says, "I am the way and the truth and the life" (John 14:6).

IN MATTHEW, CHAPTER 20, God appears as the one who takes the initiative. He goes out looking for workers. Sisters and brothers, do you think that we are here in the cathedral by our own initiative? In one sense we are because we are free, and nobody has forced us to come. But this is how God's grace works: he made us free, and he follows up our freedom with his motivating grace so that we'll use this freedom to look for him. Therefore, the initiative to come to Mass starts with God who gave us freedom and who also motivates us to do what is good. People don't come to church to hold a meeting; they come to adore God. People don't come to church out of political curiosity; they come with devotion in search of God. How wonderful it is to know that the Lord is searching for us all the hours of our lives! . . .

How rich is God in forgiveness and mercy! Before God we have no privileges or rights. If we have served God from our earliest years, then blessed be God! We have used our life well. But that doesn't give us the right to feel that we are owners of the church. Even if we are bishops, even if we are priests, we may be more in need of God's mercy than sinners who have just converted and who by their love are perhaps closer to God than those who think they own the church. God is kind. No one can judge his initiatives. Appeal to his mercy; beg like the good thief just to be remembered, and God will do more than remember you. . . .

That's what our God is like. Blessed be God who lets us know that he calls us at every hour and at every hour is ready to receive us, no matter what crimes we have committed. That is why I repeat again what I have said here so often before when by the radio I have addressed those who are responsible for so many injustices and so much violence, those who have caused weeping in so many homes, those who are stained with the blood of so many murders, those whose hands are tarnished with torture, those who have hardened their consciences and feel no pain at seeing beneath their boots so many people humiliated, suffering, perhaps near death. To all of them I say, "Your crimes do not matter. They are ugly and horrible. You have violated the highest dignity of the human person. But God calls you and forgives you."

It is perhaps here that those who see themselves as workers hired at the first hour feel disgusted and ask, "How is it that I'm going to be in heaven with those criminals?" Sisters and brothers, in heaven there are no criminals. The greatest criminals, once they have repented of their sins, are now children of God. In Jesus' time the respectable folk kept pointing at the prostitute Mary Magdalene even when she was weeping for her sins: "Look, if he were really a prophet, he would realize who that woman is who is touching him" (Luke 7:39). But Christ came to her defense: She is no longer a sinner for she has loved much and she has repented of her faults; she is already Saint Mary Magdalene (Luke 7:47). The sins of the past no longer count; they dissolve. That's why Christian justification is called rebirth. That's what Christ told Nicodemus: "If you are not born again . . ." (John 3:3). All those who repent of their faults leave behind the evil of their past lives as if shedding an old skin and donning a new one; they now have nothing to do with what was left in the past! Think of how the butterfly is born again as it leaves its cocoon and becomes a new creature. Blessed be God! This is the generosity of God.

THE REDEMPTION PLANNED BY GOD is reaching all people without any exception. It is reaching even those who feel they are sinners, those who feel that their sins are unforgivable. Who knows if my words are reaching the person whose hands are bloody with Father Grande's murder or the one who shot Father Navarro? Who knows if I'm being heard by those who have killed and tortured and done so much evil? Listen, there in your criminal hideouts! Perhaps you are already repentant. You too are called to forgiveness! Whenever I have cried out against violence, I have always added something about repentance for your sins so that you become children of God. Paul preached to the Romans, a pagan people among whom crimes and injustices abounded, but he told them, "This redemption in Christ is summoning you, but it summons you in Christ, in Christ brought by the Virgin."

This redemption is a redemption from sin, sisters and brothers, for that is what the angel told Saint Joseph, "You are to name him Jesus because he will forgive the sins of the world" (Matt. 1:21). That is the starting point of Christian liberation. When we struggle now for human rights, for freedom, for dignity; when we feel that the church's ministry means showing concern for those who are hungry, those who have no school, or those who suffer exclusion, we are not departing from God's promise. He comes to free us from sin, and the church knows that the consequences of sin are all these injustices and crimes. That is why the church knows that she is saving the world when she undertakes to speak of such things.

THIS IS A NIGHT OF TRIUMPH, a night of victory, but not a victory that leaves the enemies crushed under hatred and bloodshed. The victories achieved by bloodshed are detestable. The victories won by brute force are brutish. The victory that truly triumphs is that of faith, the victory of Christ who did not come to be served but to serve (Matt. 20:28). The triumph of his love is a peaceful triumph. Death's triumph was not definitive. The definitive victory is the triumph of life over death, the triumph of peace, the triumph of joy, the triumph of the alleluias, the triumph of the resurrection of the Lord!

But in this triumph there are two aspects, two phases. Don't forget that. The first phase is Christ's, and he is already crowned with absolute victory; he is the king of life and of eternity. Saint Paul tells us, "Christ has risen, and death has no hold on him" (Rom. 6:9). In him redemption has reached its peak. But tonight we are going to renew our baptism as Christians, and we know that for us the victory still lies ahead as the object of our hope. The banners of suffering and pain and sin and death are still raised over our world. This does not mean that Christ's death and resurrection were a failure because of human wickedness; it just means that this is the time of the church. From the resurrection of Christ until the second coming how many centuries will pass? We do not know, but we do know that with the resurrection of Christ the victory over sin and hell and death has been guaranteed and that God has asked his church to administer this victory of Christ in the hearts of every person. That is the reason for this tremendous work of evangelization, the labor of reconciling people with God, the work of bringing the blood of Christ to the hearts of all, the work of planting the love of God in the midst of hatred, the work of sowing peace among the nations, the work of promoting justice in human relationships and respect for the rights of those sanctified by the Lord's redemption.

AS LONG AS CHRIST HAD NOT RISEN, the minds of the disciples were missing a key. There was no way to explain the behavior, the doctrine, the miracles, and all the marvelous works of the Redeemer without the resurrection. Everything about Christ remained a mystery until the moment that he had often announced,

"My hour has arrived" (John 17:1). Why would he say something like that? "The Son of Man will be handed over, and they will maltreat him and crucify him, and on the third day he will rise" (Mark 9:31). They had heard his words, but they could not understand why the Son of God made man should have to undergo debasement. The disciples experienced a great crisis in their faith before they experienced this great revelation. . . .

Redemption is necessary, and it comes only by the light of the dying Christ. But the mystery becomes even more obscure when Christ ends up dead on the cross. So ends the life of the just man! Is it worthwhile being good and ending up crucified? Must we remain so passive and do without the aggressive strength that can overcome the injustices of the world by force of arms? Could not God send an army of angels to do away with all the persecutors of Jesus and his church? Such questions reveal the small-mindedness of those who want to fix the world's problems by using violence. Instead they should reflect as John did at the tomb of the risen Christ, and finally understand. For now Christ has risen; now his enemies have fled in terror. Some tried to silence the voice of the resurrection by scheming: "We'll tell people that while you guards were sleeping, they stole the body away" (Matt. 28:13). But who can cover the sun with a finger? The resurrection is a sun that is already shining.

Friday, May 18

Bishop Rivera also came to see me – a pleasant surprise – and we talked about the secret document of denunciation the other four bishops are preparing. In it, they denounce me to the Holy See in matters of faith, say I am politicized, accuse me of promoting a pastoral work with erroneous theological grounding – a whole series of accusations that completely impugn my ministry as a bishop. In spite of how serious this is, I feel great peace. I acknowledge my deficiencies before God, but I believe that I have worked with goodwill and that I am not guilty of the serious things of which they accuse me. God will have the last word on this. I am at peace and hope to continue to work with the same enthusiasm as always, since I serve the Holy Church in love.

Monday, May 21

Tonight Father Gregorio Rosa was with me, and we talked a great deal about the accusations in the document prepared by the other bishops and about the reality of our archdiocese. Father Goyo (Gregorio) thinks it is a moment of truth and that we have to use it as an opportunity to reaffirm the position of the church and remove all the obstacles that keep us from doing a more authentic pastoral work. There is some truth in their accusations, and it is necessary to correct the mistakes, but there is also a great deal of exaggeration and it is almost calumnious.

We are not going to answer it, except through our actions as we continue the pastoral work of our archdiocese.

4

The Call

THE RISEN CHRIST MUST NOW be the light for those who are creating history. The inspiration for all the laws that are set down for the people must be Christ, not the whims of the powerful. Rather, what Christ desires is the conversion of the powerful. . . .

Christ is coming. We do not await him like children expecting toys. We await him as Christians who know that he has already come, but who announced that he would come a second time to surprise us on the path of life. He will gather us up from wherever we fall dead, and we will enter with him to reign. Even now we should reign with him through our virtue and holiness.

Let us be true Christians, worthy of this eschatological hour that lasts from the first coming of Christ until the second, this final period of history.

THE MAGI ASKED, "Where is the newborn king of the Jews? For we saw his star at its rising and have come to pay him homage" (Matt. 2:2). I find in these words a wonderful expression of people who desire to be faithful to their vocation. This is the first gift that God gives, a vocation. Ask yourselves, sisters and brothers, especially you my dear young people and children: "Is this my star? Where is the full realization of my life? Where does the Lord want me?" We all have a vocation. No woman or man is born without a vocation from God. We all have a place in history, and we realize our own personalities by recognizing that place and developing ourselves there. Let us seek our happiness by always asking what God desires of us.

THE PERSON WHO DENOUNCES must be willing to be denounced. From the beginning I've said that I gladly accept criticisms when they are constructive and try to make me better than the poor soul I am. Most especially, I ask forgiveness from all those for whom my message has been misunderstood or poorly communicated. I want you to know that there is no pride or ill will in what I say; neither is there any distortion of what the gospel is ordering me to preach to this archdiocese that has been commended to my care.

The true pastor experiences this need for conversion, and he preaches it as a personal necessity for himself and for all those who want to join him in forming the authentic church of Jesus Christ. The need for conversion has been the center of the church's message about the Word of God since Christ appeared in history. It was the message of the prophets who announced him, and it was the message of ecclesial assemblies, such as the one we just experienced in Puebla. The message of the church and the attitude of genuine pastors cannot be any different. We are not God. We are fragile, limited human beings, and we need to be converted. Believe me, sisters and brothers, when I tell you that I would like to be at the head of this whole procession of conversion that our diocese is undertaking.

CONVERSION IS SOMETHING LIKE making an about-face. In the military the terms "right face" or "about face" are used for turning troops to one side or the other. Conversion means turning toward God and becoming ever more directed toward God. Christ was talking about conversion when he said, "Be perfect, just as your heavenly Father is perfect" (Matt. 5:48). When will we be perfect like God? Christ's purpose is to inspire a movement without limits, which is conversion. Conversion means asking at every moment: what does God want of my life? If God wants the opposite of what I might fancy, then doing what God wants is conversion, and following my own desire is perversion. What does God want, for example, of the political power in a country? He wants those forces to create sound laws and moral unity of will among all citizens for the common good. God does not want that power to be used to assault and to beat people or to attack cities and villages; that is perversion. What does God want of capital and of those to whom he gives money, properties, and other things? Again God seeks conversion. That means that people should bestow on the things created by God the destiny God ordains for them, which is the welfare of all, so that everyone might have a share in happiness.

FIRST OF ALL, there is an urgent need to save the dignity of persons. I can find no more beautiful example of saving human dignity than the figure of the sinless Jesus face to face with the adulterous woman who was surprised in the act and humiliated. Those who caught her want to sentence her to stoning. Without saying a word Jesus reproaches those who would judge her with their own sins, and then he asks the woman, "Has no one condemned you?" "No one, sir." "Then neither do I condemn you. But sin no more" (John 8:10–11). Strength, but tenderness. Human dignity comes first. . . .

Personal sin is at the base of the great social sin. We must keep this in mind, because today it is very easy for us to be like those who witnessed the adultery: we point it out and demand justice, but we look very little into our own consciences. How easy we find it to condemn structural injustice, institutional violence, and social sin! All that is quite real, but where are the sources of that social sin? They are in the heart of every person. Modern-day society is an anonymous society in which nobody accepts blame but everybody is responsible. All of us are responsible for what happens, but the sin remains anonymous. We are all sinners, and we have all contributed our grain of sand to this mountain of crimes and violence in our country.

That is why salvation begins with the human person, with human dignity, with freeing every individual from sin. This is God's call during Lent: let each and every one be converted! Among all of us who are here, there are not two sinners who are the same. Each of us has committed our own shameful deeds, but we want to hide them and shift the blame to others. I also am a sinner and must take off my mask. I have offended God and society, and I must ask forgiveness of God. This is the call of Christ: the human person comes first.

THERE IS TREMENDOUS ANTICIPATION, sisters and brothers. The call to conversion has awakened many hearts that were asleep in sin, like the people in Zebulun and Naphtali. These people thought that the church was meddling in politics and other areas where she had no business. Now they have finally understood that we are simply preaching the kingdom of God, which means pointing out sin in any human situation, even when the sin is found in political and economic situations. The church must be the voice of Christ; she must declare, "Be converted, for the kingdom of God is at hand" (Matt. 4:17). Those who want to enter this kingdom must draw close to God by being converted and repenting of their sins. . . . Naturally, those who are in sin must be restored to God's grace and renounce all forms of injustice and selfishness and violence. Let us become friends of God, for God has no part in sin.

THAT IS WHAT THE CHURCH WANTS: to disturb people's consciences and to provoke a crisis in their lives. A church that does not provoke crisis, a gospel that does not disturb, a word of God that does not rankle, a word of God that does not touch the concrete sin of the society in which it is being proclaimed – what kind of gospel is that? Just nice, pious considerations that bother nobody – that's the way many people would like our preaching to be. Those preachers who avoid every thorny subject so as not to bother anyone or cause conflict and difficulty shed no light on the reality in which they live. . . . Here among ourselves, sisters and brothers, we are sinners, and I am the first of them. I have offended the Lord, but, thank God, one day I heard his call pointing out my sin, and instead of becoming arrogant and closed off in my pride, instead of slandering the church because she disturbed me, I accepted instead that message of God. On that day this wayward lamb that was I – and could be any one of you – humbly drew near to the Lord and asked for forgiveness. Thankfully, there was a word that reprimanded me; there was someone who told me frankly that that was not the way to act. This is the role of the church: not to ignore the circumstances of life but to point out to people their sins so that they repent.

I AM A MINISTER OF THIS CHURCH of reconciliation, and so I was very happy with the proposal made to me that the church must not only denounce what is wrong but must also announce hope. One good reason for hope is that the church's view coincides with the views of many others, and there is therefore a need to begin a sincere dialogue among people of different opinions. I urge everyone, then, not to believe that violence is the only solution and, like Saint Paul, I call everyone to engage in sincere dialogue and to seek reconciliation in God's name.

I call upon you in the oligarchy to collaborate with the process of the people. You are the principal

protagonists in this time of change, and the cessation
of violence depends in large part on you. We said that
reconciliation is closely connected with the land. If you
recognize that you are owners of the land that belongs to
all Salvadorans, then be reconciled with God and with
your fellow citizens. Give up gladly that which will bring
peace to the people and peace to your own consciences.

THERE IS CRISIS IN THE HEART of every
Christian, and if at this moment there are any Christians
in El Salvador who do not feel this crisis, then they have
not reflected on the meaning of God's message and on
what God has sown in the world. Many have already
overcome the crisis and have committed themselves to
God's kingdom. Many have overcome it in the opposite
sense: they have settled down comfortably and find it
easier to say, "The church is communist. Why follow it?"
But some people are still in crisis; they don't know what
to do. . . . We all must decide in our own consciences
what side we will take. God our Lord is offering us
marvelous fruits if we let him sow in us that sprout
which will produce prolific branches, the fruits of eternal
life. This is God's plan, and that's why the church is the
vineyard where God's kingdom will always be in crisis.
Blessed are those who feel the crisis deeply and resolve
it by committing themselves to our Lord. I am very glad

that precisely in this hour of crisis many who were asleep have woken up and are at least asking where the truth is to be found. Look for it! Saint Paul shows us the way: it is found with prayer, reflection, and esteem for what is good. These are wonderful criteria. Wherever there is something noble, something good, something just, there we find God (Phil. 4:6–8).

IN LUKE WE HEAR how our Lord is walking through the streets of Jericho (Luke 19:1–10). In the city there is a rich man, the chief tax collector, who has an earnest desire to see Jesus. Since he is short in stature, he climbs a tree, never imagining that our Lord, cheered by the crowds, would notice him. But as he passes under the tree, he lifts his eyes, sees him, and calls him by name: "Zacchaeus, come down, for I want to go to your house. I want to stay at your house" (Luke 19:5). When Zacchaeus hears that voice, he comes down. But it is not mere curiosity that motivates him. On hearing the malicious comments of those who see Jesus enter his house, Zacchaeus shows himself to be a man who for some time has felt the weight of sin on his conscience. Before Jesus he declares: "I am going to give half my property to the poor, and if I have cheated anybody I will pay him back four times the amount." Our Lord congratulates him for that: "Zacchaeus, today happiness has come to your house."

This aspect of the gospel is very interesting because it helps us to see that true conversion expresses itself in deeds. It is not enough just to say that one repents of a sin; it is also necessary to repair the harm that was done. Since that collector of taxes and chief publican had often extorted money in carrying out his job, he felt the need to give half of his goods to the poor and to reimburse fourfold those he had defrauded. Sisters and brothers, the gospel calls us to such a conversion, a conversion that doesn't just remain in sentiments but that leads to total change and teaches us the need to share.

AND SO CHRIST ALSO SPEAKS of "those who believe in him" (John 3:18). To believe means to hand oneself over; it is not simply a matter of the head. Yes, we must believe the eternal truths, but that is not enough. Saint James says, "Even the devil believes that God exists, yet he will never be saved" (Jas. 2:19). Believing is not just something theoretical. Believing is an act of the will. Believing is Mary telling the angel, "Behold, I am the handmaid of the Lord. May it be done to me according to your word" (Luke 1:38). That is faith: handing oneself over. Faith is what a child has when her father puts out his arms and says "Jump!" and the child leaps into space with the assurance that the father's arms will not let her fall. This is faith. This is what Christ says: "Those who

believe in me will not be condemned." Those who surren-
der and do not distrust, those who even in the hardest
times believe and hope – they will not be condemned.

ALL THOSE WHO HEAR the word of God and put
it into practice are building on rock, but those who
hear the word of God only out of curiosity or literary
interest – or even worse, to find out what the bishop is
saying so they can ensnare him – are building on sand.
And when the fearful hour of God's judgment arrives,
those who want to judge me for what I am saying here
will also be judged. I do indeed fear God, and so I try
to say only what he wants me to say, even if people don't
want me to say what I'm saying.

GOD IS NOT a God we're unable to find. That is what
is most amazing. God became man and walked along
human highways in order to encounter people. In Christ
we find God's justification. Christ is the God who
pardons, the God who justifies. Christ is the God who
has come not to condemn but to forgive (John 3:17).
Christ is the shepherd who goes out in search of the lost
sheep so that they come and join in the joy of his flock of
the justified, from which no one is excluded. With what
longing he said, "I have other sheep that do not belong
to this fold, and they must be brought in" (John 10:16).

This is the heart of Jesus, the heart of God beating in a human breast. This is the infinite love of the Lord that searches all the paths of life for you and me and each one of us. No matter how far astray we go, no matter how devoid of faith we find ourselves, no matter how proud or idolatrous of the world's vanities we are, there is the Lord nearby, offering us justification and telling us it is no use to us to have lots of money, lots of power, lots of luxury if we're not converted to God. If God doesn't give you justification, then you are the poorest of the world's wretches. Without God's justification everything is mere appearance. This is the intimate justice God is offering you. In more modern language we talk of grace, forgiveness, reconciliation with God. As far as he's concerned, there is no difficulty in being reconciled with God.

Saturday, January 20

A very tragic day. It dawned with the news that there had been a military operation in El Despertar in the parish of San Antonio Abad. It was at a house frequently used for retreats. . . . Father Octavio Ortiz, along with Sister Chepita, as they call the Belgian sister who works there, was leading a program of introduction to the Christian life for some forty young men. But at dawn today, the National Guard with a riot squad set off a bomb to break down the door and then entered violently with armored cars and shooting. Father Octavio, when he realized what was happening, got up only to meet his death, as did four other young men. The rest of the group, including two women religious, were taken to the headquarters of the National Guard. . . .

In the evening, this tragic funereal cortege was taken to the cathedral. A great many people were there; the cathedral was almost full. There were many prayers for

the slain and gospel messages preached to the crowd. I
got there at about eleven p.m. . . . I led an intercessory
prayer for Father Octavio and the others and also
explained to the crowd how we would proceed the
next day. I invited all of them to come to the eight
a.m. Mass at the cathedral. All the priests will be there,
having suspended their normal Sunday schedules to
concelebrate this Mass for their brother priest.

5

The Way

WHEN WE LIVE LIVES CENTERED on God, then
God is the center of our life, and our relations with
others derive from God. When my use of the things God
has created derives from God as the center that inspires
my ethics, then I will be moral, honorable, and honest;
I will tell the truth, I will not distort the news; I will
not spread calumny because I know that God will hold
me accountable. When God is the center of our lives,
as Saint Paul says, then we will "pursue righteousness,
devotion, love, faith, patience, and gentleness; we will
struggle hard for the faith" (1 Tim. 6:11–12).

My sisters and brothers, this struggle of faith in which
we are engaged is not a struggle of arms or of violence
but of ideas and convictions. We do violence first to
ourselves by the inspiration of faith according to what
Saint Paul says so beautifully: "I insist that you keep the
commandment without stain or reproach" (1 Tim. 6:14).
The commandment is the whole body of things that God

has revealed and commanded, and we as servants of God have an obligation to obey. But when we shake off God's yoke and no longer hear God speaking in our conscience, then we have the situation where each person wants to be a god. The result of this is a cataclysm, as if the sun and the planets revolving around it were to lose their center of gravity and crash into one another. The sun is God, and as long as we revolve around God with an ethic that looks to God, then we will live together as sisters and brothers.

WE GIVE THANKS because the church, the people of God in this community, is passing through what we have called an hour of cross and of Easter. The cross is in the pain of persecution. The cross is in the murder of priests who died this year. They should not have died; they should still be working with us, but now we number them among the dead, not by the will of God but by the crimes of human beings. The cross is in the persecution that we experience this year in the many empty posts where no priest is present. The cross is in the fear that exists in the communities that reflect on the word of God, just as there was in the early days when people imagined that Christianity was threatening the established peace. "The days will come," said Christ as he lamented the time when people would believe that they were serving God by killing Christians (John 16:2).

WE WANT PEACE, but not the peace of violence and of cemeteries, not peace imposed or extorted. We want peace that is the fruit of justice, peace that is the fruit of obedience to God, for God was expecting the righteousness and justice that his vineyard should have produced but got in return only murders. What we have of humanity and Christianity in El Salvador *should* have produced much peace, much right, much justice. How different our country would be if it were producing what God has planted here! It's sad to say, but God feels he has failed with certain societies, and I think that the passages from Isaiah and Saint Paul that we read today have become a very sad Salvadoran reality: "I looked for righteousness, and behold, murders! I looked for justice, and behold, laments!" (Isa. 5:7).

We are not planting discord with these. We are simply crying out to the God who is weeping, to the God who hears the laments of his people because there is so much violence, to the God who feels the distress of his campesinos who cannot sleep in their homes because they must spend their nights in flight. God hears the wailing of the children who cry out for their parents who have disappeared: Where are they?

AH! IF ONLY WE HAD PEOPLE of prayer among those who manage the destiny of the country and the

destiny of the economy! If only they relied more on God
and his techniques rather than on their own human technology, we would have a world that the church dreams
about, a world without injustices, a world respectful of
rights, a world where all people generously participate,
a world without repression, a world without torture.
Forgive me if I always mention torture, but there is a
heaviness in my poor spirit when I think about those
people who suffer the scourges, the kicks, and the blows
of another human being. If they had just a bit of God in
their hearts, they would see a brother or sister as an image
of God. I say this because these situations continue. The
arrests and the "disappearances" continue. How I hope
that a little contact with God will change these dungeons
of hell, that a little light will shine on them and make
those running them understand what God desires of
them. God does not want those things. God repudiates
evil. God wants what is good, what is love.

"YOU HAVE NOT KEPT to my paths but have been
partial to persons in applying the law," says the prophet
(Mal. 2:9). If they're Mr. So-and-so or Mrs. So-and-so,
then we hear, "Happy to do it!" But if they're some poor,
despicable persons, they're almost ignored. The church
of the poor is a criterion of authenticity because she is
not a church of classes. That doesn't mean despising the

rich, but it does mean telling the rich that, if they don't become poor in their hearts, they will not be able to enter the kingdom of heaven. The true preacher of Christ is the church of the poor that looks to the God who hears those who are praying in the poverty and misery and pain of the slums in the hope that they will be heard. Only by drawing close to those voices can the church feel close to God. "You are partial to persons in applying the law." How well the campesinos put it: "The law is like a snake; it bites only those who walk barefoot."

WE HAVE A MESSAGE to communicate to the world, and we are the ones responsible for this message. When Christ chose twelve men to receive his divine wisdom, he told them finally, "I have much more to tell you, but you cannot bear it now (John 16:12–13). The deposit of divine revelation that I offer you is so great that my divine Spirit will be with you. You are chosen from the people and will have God's special assistance so that in every moment throughout history you will preach my word according to the needs of the times. You must incarnate my word in the needs and the sins and the virtues of the people you have in your charge." This is the great ministry of the word. It is so difficult and so incomprehensible that often the dialogue that the church wishes to establish to enlighten the world turns into persecution. Sometimes the offenses against the ministry of the word become as terrible as the ones we are suffering at the present time. "He came to his own," we can say, "and the light shone, but the darkness did not want to receive it" (John 1:11, 5). This is the mystery of iniquity, the mystery of sin that the church attempts to root out from the world and from history, even as history and the world attempt to suffocate the word of God.

Therefore, my brother priests, you have arrived at the height of priestly ordination in order to proclaim this word which, like the prophets, you feel burning deep within you, a devouring flame from which we would just as soon flee. I speak of this ministry not as an honor but as a prophetic duty, for we are called to go forth and proclaim the authentic revelation to the people.

Dear brothers, do not betray your service to this ministry of God's word. It is very easy to be servants of the word without disturbing the world in any way. We can spiritualize our words so that they lack any commitment to history. We can speak words that sound good in any part of the world because they say nothing about the world. Such words create no problems; they give rise to no conflicts. The word that characterizes the authentic church is the word that causes conflicts and persecutions. It is the searing word of the prophets that announces and denounces: it announces the marvelous works of God so that people will believe and worship God, and it denounces the sins of those who oppose God's kingdom. The true word denounces sins so that they will be uprooted from people's hearts, from their societies, from their laws, and from all those organizations that oppress and imprison and trample upon the rights of God and humankind.

This is the difficult service of the word, but the Spirit of God accompanies the prophet and the preacher because it is through them that Christ himself continues to proclaim his kingdom to men and women of every era.

THERE CAN BE NO FREEDOM as long as there is sin in the heart. What's the use of changing structures? What's the use of violence and armed force if the motivation is hatred and the purpose is to buttress those in power or else to overthrow them and then create new tyrannies? What we seek in Christ is true freedom, the freedom that transforms the heart, the freedom the risen Christ announces to us today, "Seek what is above" (Col. 3:1). Don't view earthly freedom and the oppression of this unjust system in El Salvador just by looking down from the rooftops. Look on high! That doesn't mean accepting the situation, because Christians also know how to struggle. Indeed, they know that their struggle is more forceful and valiant when it is inspired by this

Christ who knew how to do more than turn the other cheek and let himself be nailed to a cross. Even submitting to crucifixion, he has redeemed the world and sung the definitive hymn of victory, the victory that cannot be used for other ends but benefits those who, like Christ, are seeking the true liberation of human beings.

This liberation is incomprehensible without the risen Christ, and it's what I want for you, dear sisters and brothers, especially those of you who have such great social awareness and refuse to tolerate the injustices in our country. It's wonderful that God has given you this keen sensibility, and if you have a political calling, then blessed be God! Cultivate it well, and be careful not to lose that vocation. Don't replace that social and political sensitivity with hatred, vengeance, and earthly violence. Lift your hearts on high, and consider the things that are above!

THOSE WHO PREACH and inspire the various forms of earthly liberation do not have to be ideologues, much less atheists who are without God and without Christ. The one who most inspires the liberation of our country and of humanity is the one and only liberator, the risen Christ. Christ is the one who proclaims this morning the true victory over all the oppressive forces of the earth. This Christ who now reigns in the glory of the

Father can challenge the might of Pontius Pilate and the Roman Empire; he can defy the fanaticism of the spiritual leaders of Israel, the priests who have perverted the meaning of religion. By his resurrection Christ offers all the liberators of earth this challenge: "You will not free people! The only liberation that endures is that which breaks the chains on the human heart, the chains of sin and selfishness." Christ is the one who has left the grave empty and has broken through the bars of death and hell, and now he invites all men and women to die happily so that they also, at the hour of the universal resurrection, can defy the tombs of our cemeteries, saying, "Death, where is your victory?" (1 Cor. 15:55)

Everything else dies, everything else is sin, everything else is hatred and violence, everything else is bloodshed and murder and kidnapping. None of that is liberation. All that is buried among the old things that Christ leaves behind to give us the new, true life which only true Christians can experience. Let us hope that the fanatics of violence and terrorism, as well as those who think repression and force are going to fix the situation, learn that those are not the ways of the Lord. Rather, the ways of the Lord are love and respect and obeying the law of the Lord; they are the humble ways of Christ. Christ is the one who grants true liberation to those who want to accept it. Christ is indeed the key to the revelation of God.

The Way

IN ALL OF HISTORY no one has ever encountered a love that was so – how to say it? – so crazy, so exaggerated: giving to the point of being crucified on a cross. There is no friend who has given his life for another friend with such an outpouring of suffering and love as Christ our Lord. . . . That is why Christ tells us that the sign of the Christian is living the new commandment he gives us. It is a commandment that tonight becomes fresh in our memory and our lives: "As I have loved you, so you also should love one another" (John 13:34).

This is the greatest disease of our world today: not knowing how to love. Everything is selfishness. Everything is exploitation of human beings. Everything is cruelty and torture. Everything is violence and repression. The houses of our people are burned. Our sisters and brothers are thrown into prison and tortured. So many cruel acts are committed against them. Jesus, how you must suffer tonight as you behold the situation of our nation with all its many crimes and cruelties! I see Christ saddened as he sits at his Passover supper and looks upon El Salvador; he tells us, "I told you to love one another." . . .

Dear young people given to violence and vice, you who have already lost your faith in love and think that love can solve nothing, here is the proof that love alone solves everything. If Christ had wanted to impose his redemption through armed force or through fire and violence, he would have achieved nothing. That would have been useless; there would be only more hatred and wickedness. But going straight to the heart of redemption, Christ tells us on this night, "This is my commandment: as I have loved you, so you also should love one another." And he says more: "So that you may see that these are not simply words, stay with me tonight when I will sweat blood as I observe the evil of human-kind and the pain of my own sufferings! And tomorrow you will see me carrying the cross like a silent lamb and dying on Calvary. Be assured that I bear no resentment toward anybody. From the depth of my soul I will cry out, 'Father, forgive them, they know not what they do'" (Luke 23:34). Let us reflect, sisters and brothers, on this personified gesture of love. And when we are tempted to act with vengeance, resentment, cruelty, or selfishness, let us not consider the sad example of people who hate one another. Rather let us raise our eyes toward the love that becomes lamb, that becomes food, that becomes Passover, that becomes covenant. . . .

Only by humility can we be redeemers and collabora-tors in the true collaboration that the world needs. Liberation that cries out against others is not true liberation. No liberation brings true freedom if it causes hateful, violent revolutions that destroy the lives and offend the dignity of people. True freedom is that which does violence to itself just as Christ, almost disregarding his sovereign power, becomes a slave in order to serve others. These are the true liberators that this tremendous hour demands of our country, liberators with humble hearts in which Christian love shines bright.

HOW BEAUTIFUL IS THE GREETING of the risen Christ: "Peace be with you" (John 20:19, 21, 26). That is his gift: peace. That is why any people that riddles peace with bullets – it's sad to say it – is not a Christian people. In those zones of repression and hostility where the greeting of peace sounds sarcastic, El Salvador is the antichrist. My dear sisters and brothers of Perulapán, my hope is that all of you without distinction fall on your knees before Christ, who alone gives peace. Peace does not come from military operations with the collaboration of ORDEN, nor does peace come from the revenge carried out by some popular organization. Peace comes only from Christ. Only by believing in Christ and in one another can we ever experience true peace.

Sunday, February 10

During the Mass, which was held at the basilica because the cathedral continues to be occupied, I received a warm reception after my trip. I felt a special affection in that church, which was very full; the crowd continued to swell as the Mass progressed. The homily went on for almost two hours. I think I may be going on too long, but I feel, even so, the need to guide these people, who are listening to me avidly. I talk for so long precisely because I do not see my audience tiring; they seem always attentive. I hear that they also follow the radio broadcast with the same attention. . . .

I went to have lunch and spend the afternoon with the sisters from the hospital, who came to the house of the Oblate Sisters of Divine Love, and with the sisters from the Colegio de la Sagrada Familia, who also came. We enjoyed a very nice familial atmosphere, which strengthens our efforts for a church that, in its difficult struggles, must also feel the tenderness of the

love God has always given us in order to strengthen
our work for the kingdom.

Tuesday, February 12

A group of students celebrating the victory won in the
Ministry of Education was holding a demonstration,
which was broken up violently by certain elements
of the right along with the army, which followed
the disbanded crowd until it entered the Christian
Democrats' building, which is occupied by the Popular
Leagues of February 28. There gunfire left several
dead and many wounded.

The committee of Christian Democrats came to ask me
to give asylum in the seminary to two women, members
of the Leagues who were occupying the Christian
Democrats' headquarters, who came out in the guise
of liberated hostages. One of these women saw her own
husband fall dead during the gunfire and is extremely
nervous. We managed to arrange for them to go to the
Colegio de la Sagrada Familia.

6

The Church

CHRIST TELLS US, "I will not leave you orphans. I will
return. In a little while the world will no longer see me,
but you will see me because I live and you will live" (John
14:18–20). I am going to repeat this phrase which may
seem puzzling, and yet it is the most sublime revelation
of our Christianity: "I, Christ, am in the Father, and you
are in me and I in you." Look at this beautiful chain!
"Whoever has my commandments and observes them
is the one who loves me. And whoever loves me will be
loved by my Father, and I will love him and reveal myself
to him" (John 14:21).

What does this mean? It is the most sublime revelation. Your life as a worker, your life as a poor person
living in a cardboard house, your life as a rich man living
in a palace – your life has no meaning unless it becomes
part of this flow that identifies it with Christ, because
when united with Christ, you are with God and God
is with you. This is Christ's dynamic; this is the divine
energy of the Spirit.

It would seem that the church, after twenty centuries of so many persecutions and so much fury directed against her, should already have disappeared. In El Salvador it should already have been wiped out. But the dynamism and the strength of the church is not in us human beings who can be very fragile and very sinful. I am not surprised when people criticize me because of my sins – I know I am sinful. Who is not sinful? But those who look at the speck in another's eye so often forget the beam that is in their own eye. They should first remove the beam from their own eyes, the dung from their own vision, so that they do not look upon others with the same blurred vision. We must have this perspective: the church as a human institution would simply not continue in existence, but the church persists because she is composed of people who place their fragile trust in Christ, and Christ is in God, and God is in Christ and in us. This is a current that travels from earth to heaven through Christ, and through Christ it comes back down to earth bringing with it the Spirit of God, the Spirit of truth, the Spirit of strength.

SAINT PAUL TELLS the Thessalonians, "Do not quench the Spirit! Do not despise the gift of prophecy. Test everything; retain what is good" (1 Thess. 5:19–21). What does it mean not to quench the Spirit? This word awakens in me a great sense of responsibility as bishop and pastor because I know that the Spirit of God – the Spirit that created the body of Christ in the womb of Mary, the Spirit that is creating the church in history here in the archdiocese – is a Spirit that is hovering over a new creation, as it says in Genesis (Gen. 1:2). I sense that there is something new happening in the archdiocese. I am a fragile, limited man, and I don't know what's happening, but I do know that God knows. And my role as pastor is just what Saint Paul is telling me today: "Do not quench the Spirit." If I peremptorily order a priest, "Don't do that!" or if I arrogantly command a community, "Don't go that way!" and in so doing try to set myself up as if I were the Holy Spirit trying to shape the church to my liking, then I would be quenching the Spirit. . . .

Do you remember when Christ received the visit of a pagan centurion? When Christ told him, "I will go cure your servant," the centurion very humbly and confidently said to him, "No, Lord, I am not worthy to have you go there. Just say one word, and my servant will be healed." Christ was amazed, says the Gospel, and exclaimed, "In truth, I have not found faith this great in Israel." Now let me tell you something. Christ will also say about this church: "Perhaps there is more faith and holiness outside the limits of Catholicism." That is why we must not quench the Spirit: the Spirit knows no borders. The Spirit is not monopolized by any Christian movement or by any hierarchy or priesthood or by any religious congregation. The Spirit is free and wants all people, wherever they are found, to fulfill their vocation of encountering Christ, the Christ who became flesh to save all human flesh. And yes, I'm aware, sisters and brothers, that even people who have lost their faith or who are not Christians come to this cathedral – they are welcome! If my words say something to them, then I invite them to reflect on them in the intimacy of their conscience because I can tell them, as Christ would, "The kingdom of God is not far from you! God's kingdom is within your heart! Seek it, and you will find it!" (Luke 17:21).

WHAT DID THAT SPIRIT give the newborn community of eleven apostles? The traitor was no longer there, but he would soon be replaced by another, and still others would succeed the apostles, and these would eventually become this community of ours which today fills the cathedral and is listening to us through the radio. We are the community that, by the promise and breath of Christ, has received the Spirit: "Receive the Holy Spirit." With that breath of Christ the church was born, as Christ himself explained, "As the Father has sent me, so I send you" (John 20:21–22). The mission that the church carries out in the world for all ages is none other than the mission of Christ dead and risen. The church celebrates her liturgy and preaches her word for that reason alone: to save people from sin, to save them from enslavements, to overthrow idolatries, and to proclaim the one God who loves us. This will always be the difficult task of the church, and she realizes that she must never betray his message. Since carrying out this mission cost Christ humiliation and the cross, the church also must be ready if necessary to suffer martyrdom, the cross, humiliation, and persecution, as Christ did.

IT IS OUR OWN CHURCH COMMUNITY that is singing today's first reading: "I overflow with joy in the Lord, and I rejoice with my God because he has clothed me magnificently and has wrapped me in a mantle of triumph" – what a comparison! – "like a bridegroom wearing a crown or a bride bedecked in her jewels" (Isa. 61:10). It's a beautiful thing to see a young man and woman who love one another approaching the altar in their finest clothes. They hand themselves over to love. It is this comparison from the Old Testament that God uses to describe this pact between the God who wants to save us and the people who need salvation.

GOD WANTS TO SAVE US as a people. He does not want to save each of us in isolation. That is why the church today more than ever before emphasizes what it means to be a "people." And that is why the church experiences conflicts: the church does not want just crowds; she wants a people. A crowd is a bunch of individuals, and the more lethargic they are, the better; the more conformist they are, the better. The church rejects the communist propaganda that religion is the opium of the people. She has no intention of being the opium of the people. It is others who drug the people and put them to sleep, and they are happy to keep them that way.

The church wants to rouse men and women to the true meaning of being a people. What does it mean to be a people? A people is a community of persons in which everyone works together for the common good.

THE VOCATION OF HUMAN BEINGS is to collaborate in the salvation of others. This is also the sense of the parable that was read today: "The kingdom of heaven is like the yeast that a woman put into the dough so that the whole batch was leavened" (Matt. 13:33). This is what being a Christian means, according to Christ: being leaven. Bakers know how the little bit of yeast that is placed within the dough leavens the entire mass. This is what Christians should be: the smidgens of yeast that go on to transform their families, their neighborhoods, their communities, their towns, the entire country, the entire world! But now we are yeast without strength, and that is why we have not been able to leaven the mass. This reflection should help us, then, to understand the responsibilities we have by our Christian vocation to be apostles and to be the leaven of our society.

PAUL THEN WENT with his group of Christians to the house of their friend Jason, and the authorities pursued them there, wanting to try them before the people. They shouted to the magistrates, "These Christians have been turning the world upside down. Now they have come here, and Jason has given them lodging. They go against the decrees of Caesar and claim that there is another king named Jesus" (Acts 17:6–7). What do you think of this, sisters and brothers? It's just like what they're saying about us now, "They are subversives. They are against authority. They should be put in prison." There is nothing strange in this . . . for the history of our communities is the history of persecution. Christians have always proclaimed that Jesus is truly King and Lord, and they have always proclaimed that his gospel is the one and only word of salvation. And whenever Christians have used the word of God to denounce the abuses of worldly power, persecutions have arisen.

According to the Book of Acts, they arrested the Christians, but they let Jason go free on bond (Acts 17:9). Later, in his letter to the Thessalonians, Saint Paul wrote the wonderful words of praise you just heard: "You have not allowed yourselves to be overcome by these difficulties, and from your community the word of the Lord has resonated throughout the world. You have believed in the living God" (1 Thess. 1:8–9). So you see? This is the community of life. This is the church, a communion of life. And that's the reason why we come together now in the cathedral, in our country chapels, and in all our Christian gatherings. It's not to commemorate someone who's dead! What a sorry lot are those Christians who think that their religion is a museum of memories; their only desire is to preserve the memories and not expose themselves to danger. No, sisters and brothers, the church is communion and life; she is communion of life, and her members must confront life in real time. That is life. The church's laws, dogmas, and beliefs must be transformed into life. Those who don't want to understand the church this way are not worshiping the eternal living One, Christ, who will never die. We worship a living God who walks alongside the people, the God who tells us not to commit injustices because if the poor victims of usurers and loan sharks "cry out to heaven, I will hear them, for I am the living God" (Exod. 22:27).

IF YOU WANT TO HEAR a message of joy and optimism, read Saint Luke. Read about the joy with which
the disciples announced the good news, telling people
that God has come and that sinners and outcasts and
everyone who needs good news could find it there in the
gospel, a word that means "good news." In this same way
our own church becomes a community that transmits
Christ, a community that continues the homily that is
Christ in a particular style. This is also marvelous: each
community, each preacher, each catechist, each religious
congregation, each element of the church has its own
charism, its own way of being, so that we can recount,
among all of us, the marvelous truth that Christ lives
through his Spirit in us. . . .

And so I repeat what I told you once before, precisely
when we were afraid that one day we would be without
the radio: the best microphone of God is Christ, and the
best microphone of Christ is the church, and the church
is all of you! Each one of you, from your own position
and your own vocation, should live the faith intensely
whether you are married, a religious, a bishop, a priest,
a student, an undergrad, a laborer, a worker, a market
vendor. In your own particular situation you should feel
that you are a true microphone of God our Lord. . . . If
the day comes when the forces of evil leave us without
this marvelous medium, which they themselves possess

in abundance while leaving the church to fight for the scraps, let us be assured that they will not have hurt us. To the contrary, we will then be even mightier microphones of the Lord and we will proclaim his word far and wide.

HOW MUCH GOODNESS, how much truth, how much honesty there is beyond our Christian borders! Let us respect this, because often we think that we're the best there is in the world just because we're in the church. Who knows? Who knows whether those of us in the church are in fact less good, less noble, and less human than those outside the church who are already prepared for the gospel and are waiting with a nobility that is truly worthy of receiving Christianity? The gospel will then reach that fertile earth Saint Paul speaks of, "all that is good, all that is noble, pure, gracious, and just" (Phil. 4:8). None of this is wasted, sisters and brothers. All of this is preparation for the gospel, and that's why we should not be fanatics! Fanaticism among Christians has caused much damage. It is like the arrogance of the elder son who points to the prodigal and says, "That one is bad. I am good" (Luke 15:25–30). In reality, the one who was good was the prodigal son who returned repentant to give his father his rueful love; it was not the brother who was smug in his phony, hypocritical fidelity.

THE DAY WHEN WE UNDERSTAND this universal work of the church – this mission of carrying the message of salvation to all the world, a mission God has entrusted to our people – divisions will disappear because of the universal demands upon us. I called upon our Protestant sisters and brothers to struggle to unite instead of sowing more sects and making Christianity more divided. We as Protestants and Catholics are giving a horrible witness by being so divided, and more so you Protestants for being divided into so many sects, all of them calling themselves Christian and all professing the Bible. It is as if Christ were divided, says Saint Paul (1 Cor. 1:13). We have the obligation to unite in his message by rooting out our selfishness and our individualist ways of thinking. Only in this way will we present the one faith in the one Christ and form the one flock that will save the whole world. . . .

We journey toward the same destiny; we are crew members on the same ship; and it is the same beacon with the same light that guides our common ship in the midst of the storms of time and life.

THE CHURCH HAS INSPIRED great hope in our hearts precisely because she no longer finds her power in worldly realities and because she is now lacking the support that people offer her out of self-interest. She has learned to be free of all that in order to be faithful to the Gospel. Now in her poverty the church knows that she is with the poor, and all those who want to live with her and share her hopes must find support in the weakness of the derided Christ, in the weakness of the church as spouse of Christ, in her poverty, in her gospel, and in her authentic following of the Lord. . . .

Let us preserve this hope, not only the hope that the church will continue working in all her authenticity, beauty, and unity, but also the hope that this church, made more beautiful in persecution, may be understood by the persecutors themselves to be free of hatred and resentment. May the church know how to apply all the rich potential that Christ offers her to sanctifying family life, to sanctifying politics, to sanctifying the economy, and to making it possible for Christ to say, also in El Salvador, "The kingdom of God is near. Be converted!" (Mark 1:15).

Thursday, February 14

I went to Domus Mariae and in Sister Maria's house, as I had promised before my trip, I met with those priests who have been identified as being most linked with the left. . . . . I used the opportunity to express my fears and to insist that, amid the fluctuations of politics and of our affinity for the popular political organizations, we truly be signs of the kingdom of God, because this is why we are in the church: to give witness of a transcendent presence amid our work on earth. They offered their comments, according to the gospel, on this thinking. I will continue to ask God for them to be, as the bishop of Brugge said to me in Belgium, not enemies or victims, but true collaborators.

In the afternoon, an interesting meeting with representatives of the popular organizations. There was one representative of the UDN political party and another from the Popular Leagues of February 28. The other two, FAPU and the Popular Revolutionary Bloc, could not come, because they were delayed at the last minute — possibly because the funerals of the victims of yesterday's repression were at the same time.

But this conversation . . . . was fruitful. I had the chance to express my concerns and to point out the areas of competence of the church, to defend the Christian sentiments of the people, and to search, all of us, as true Salvadorans, for the most peaceful and honorable solution to this crisis in our country.

We agreed to continue these meetings and that the church would offer its services without ever losing its identity as church. . . . I said that it must be clear that we would not take part as a political force, but rather as church, with the light of the gospel. It seems that this clarification was beneficial and that there is a new aspect to our relationship with these organizations.

7

The Kingdom

ISAIAH PRESENTS US WITH a beautiful panorama
(Isa. 60:1–6). Darkness covers the earth, confusion reigns
in the world where God has not shed his light. Then in
Jerusalem the people behold a light, not a light coming
from outside, but rather a God who becomes incarnate in
Jerusalem and makes Jerusalem a light that illuminates
the paths of history and the world. Along these roads
illumined by God travel all the world's peoples, bringing
their tribute so as to form one single kingdom, the
kingdom of God. . . . He did not create different races and
peoples so that they would be confounded by their diversity of languages and unable to understand one another,
nor did he create social diversity so as to marginalize
some people while others lived well. What God wanted
was to make the whole world a great community.

CHRIST IS ALREADY BUILDING this kingdom;
we human beings are not going to do this by ourselves.

We have heard the beautiful description of Isaiah when he refers to Christ our Lord: "A child is born to us; a son is given to us; upon his shoulders dominion rests. They name him Wonder-Counselor, God-Hero, Father-Forever, Prince of Peace. His dominion is vast and forever peaceful, from David's throne, and over his kingdom, which he confirms and sustains by judgment and justice . . ." (Isa. 9:6–7).

In our days the church has been given the responsibility to criticize and analyze the kingdoms of earth and bring people to an awareness that they are still lacking in justice and peace and effectiveness. Only when Christ, the true king announced by God, becomes truly the king of all hearts will the reign that God desires become a reality. The ideal king did not appear on the throne of David until that night when the angels sang the words of the prophet: "For a child is born, and upon his shoulders is the reign of peace and justice and love."

THE CHURCH IS NOT on earth to gain privileges, to seek support in power and wealth, or to ingratiate herself with the mighty of the world. The church does not exist even to erect great material temples or monuments. The church is not on the earth to teach the wisdom of the earth. The church is the kingdom of the God who is giving us every opportunity to be divine children. The ones who are great in the kingdom of the church are those who live in holiness (Matt. 13:43). . . . The only true persons are those who do not fear anything on earth because they fear one thing alone: losing God's friendship. Preserving that friendship with God is their only treasure. All other friendships are viewed as unimportant when God tells them, as he told his friend Abraham, "You are my friend. You are my child. As coheir with Christ, you're destined to possess my kingdom, my happiness. I will be your reward" (Rom. 8:17).

THERE IS NO LONGER DISTINCTION between Jew and Gentile (Gal. 3:28). There is no longer a privileged people and a marginalized people. All of us are coheirs in the mystery of Christ. The inheritance of God our Father is for all of us who are sisters and brothers. Christ, the elder brother and heir of all the promises, makes us his sisters and brothers; he makes us "coheirs," a word invented by Saint Paul. That "co-" indicates an equality that can be expressed only in terms of two equal siblings who receive the same inheritance, becoming coheirs of all that God has promised.

In Christ all human beings are called to this wealth of God's kingdom. We are members of the same body. In all his theology Saint Paul develops the meaning of this equality which makes all of us members of one body.

God did not make us to live dispersed and separated. We need one another. The head can never tell the feet, "I don't need you." The hands cannot tell the heart it's unnecessary, nor can the heart say that to the other members. All the members, each in its proper function, are members of the living body (1 Cor. 12:12–26).

WHEN THE WISE MEN CAME from the East . . . a star knew how to guide them to where the shepherds and the humble folk had found the one they were looking for (Matt. 2:1–2). So also, the wise and the rich must become humble and simple like the magi who came from the East to offer gold, frankincense, and myrrh to the child Jesus. Wealth also has a place beside the manger of the child Jesus, but only when placed there by the humble hands of the shepherds and the magi.

THERE MUST HAVE BEEN a moment of frustration, I would guess, when Christ saw the great crowds that followed him, but among them only simple people, only peasants and fishermen. If perchance some learned persons drew near, Christ perhaps saw them withdraw with disdain, laughing at the teaching of that crazy preacher. And so when Christ was left all alone, he raised his eyes to his Father and expressed the tenderness, the anguish, the affliction of his heart: "Father, why do those people refuse to believe this wonderful teaching I offer them while others, especially the simple folk, accept it from me? I give you thanks, Father, for you have hidden these things from the learned and proud and have revealed them to simple people. Yes, Father, thus you have willed" (Matt. 11:25–26). The initiative is God's. Jesus Christ is not to blame; neither is the church or the preacher. And if some people want to sneer because only the simple folk follow us, then here in the Gospel we find the explanation. . . .

When Christ was entering Jerusalem mounted on a donkey, he seems to be a mock king, but he is the king who saves. Envisioning this king mounted on a burro, the prophet proclaims, "This man comes to destroy the chariots, the horses, the warriors' bows. He is the one who will bring peace to all peoples" (Zech. 9:10). In similar fashion, the Gospel contrasts the multitude of simple folk with the learned and the self-sufficient, those who are great in the world's eyes. It is not God who rejects any class of persons or prefers one or another class. It is we who elect ourselves or segregate ourselves. Those who accept the word of God elect themselves and belong to the worthy remnant of Israel. Those who in their pride think that the church and Christ are preaching foolishness segregate themselves; they justify everything, describing our teaching with repugnant epithets and saying it is not worthy of the wise of this world. That is why the children of the Beatitudes are the poor and the humble.

WITH THE COMING OF CHRIST, God has injected himself into history. With the birth of Christ the kingdom of God is inaugurated in human time. Every year for twenty centuries now, we remember this night when the kingdom of God arrived in the world, this night when Christ inaugurated the fullness of time. His birth signifies that God is walking with humans in history; we are not alone on our journey. We can hope for peace and justice and a kingdom of divine right; we can hope for something holy and far beyond earthly realities, not because we humans can create this blessing proclaimed by God's sacred words but because God is already in the midst of humanity, building a kingdom of justice and love and peace.

THE LIGHT OF GOD should shed light on this struggle of the church and this renewal in Christ. Our hope is that this earth, even if it is not paradise, still in some way will reflect the reality of paradise. The kingdom of God, which will be perfect only in eternity, must nevertheless be reflected in our relations here on earth because such matters cannot simply be improvised. The citizen of heaven must first be a good citizen on earth. Those who want to take part in the promises of eternity must collaborate with God in justice and peace and love in this kingdom of earth. And so, sisters and brothers, the struggle of the church is precisely to sow more love, to awaken greater hope, to help sinners repent of their sins and draw closer to God, and to renew us all interiorly.

THIS YEAR IS ENDING, and as time passes we turn toward the God who blessed the people who believed in him: "May the Lord bless you and keep you. May he let his face shine upon you and show you favor. May the Lord look upon you and give you peace" (Num. 6:24–27). What a beautiful promise to hear at the conclusion of the year! Invoking the name of God is a classical biblical expression. It does not mean calling upon God only with our lips; it means becoming aware that we are God's people. It means that God's church is committed to the history of humanity. Invoking God's name on the people means that these people have a commitment to God so that they give glory to God as they journey through history not only by expressing fine sentiments but by creating a society that is truly the society of God's children. They must create a society where peace is not only a balance of fear, where peace is not simply the silence of cemeteries, but where peace is the joyful dynamic of a God of peace. As a God of peace he builds; he pours himself out, we might say, in goodness; he brings about the manifold marvels of creation. And as God's children we must do the same: we must create a peace that is built upon justice, love, and goodness.

ISAIAH ANNOUNCED, six centuries before the event, what the church founded by the Redeemer would be like (Isa. 66:18–21). He spoke of how all the world's peoples would come to Jerusalem. This would be the sign of the kingdom of God, a sign that passed on to the church founded by Christ. To those who came from distant lands and the ends of the earth God gave an order: "Go out to all the world and preach the gospel" (Mark 16:15). The list of places begins in Isaiah: "Tarshish, Ethiopia, Libya, Mosoch, Tubal, Greece, and even the distant coastlands that have never heard of my fame." It is almost as if we heard here about the coasts of America that were discovered sixteen centuries after these words were pronounced. Or as if we heard here the very names of this church that now is on pilgrimage. It is the same as when I mentioned today Tenancingo, San Sebastián in Ciudad Delgado, El Carmen, and all those parishes and communities of the villages where people are gathered together in reflection. These names are being strung together as pearls of God's kingdom. To all these peoples and communities the kingdom must be brought.

IF WE ARE REASONABLE in our hopes for a world where we will love one another as children of God and where there will be no enmity or violence or rancor, then we must work to make these qualities a part of our history here and now on earth. Everyone must contribute, especially those who have in their hands the ability to transform a nation: the government officials, the wealthy, and the powerful. They have a greater obligation to reflect this hope and this faith. We are the little flock of the church's history, the humblest of El Salvador's social groups. The church is worth little in terms of money or politics but has great value because of the hope in the hearts of her children. The poorest campesino and the humblest woman of the village, simply by living this hope and this faith, by praying to God, by educating their children, and by bearing witness to their hope, are equal collaborators with the powerful in the construction of the kingdom of God that Christ wants on this earth. This kingdom of God has come already – it is in your hearts!

THE PROPHET ISAIAH says that God's kingdom will come to break "the rod of the taskmaster." The yoke was the symbol of subjugated people who were placed under a heavy burden. God will break this yoke and give the people freedom. Those oppressed will sing with joy because God has visited them and saved them. My brothers and sisters, this is how God acts when he becomes present among people; he destroys the yokes and the rods of the oppressors. This is what every man and woman, every family and every people, ought to cry out for when they feel humiliated, afflicted, and depressed like the people of Zebulun and Naphtali: there is reason to hope!

The prophet was not deceived. Something began to change on earth when Christ appeared in those lands curing the sick, raising the dead, preaching to the poor, bringing hope to the people. It was like when a stone is cast into a quiet lake – ripples appear, and they spread until they reach the shores. Christ appeared in Zebulun and Naphtali with the same signs of liberation: he broke the oppressive yokes, he brought joy to the hearts of people, and he sowed hope in their hearts. This is what God is doing now in history.

That is why the church insists on preaching this joyful presence of God in history. Let no one destroy this joy, sisters and brothers. Let us all experience the love with which God visits us, for God truly loves us. Even though he sometimes permits the humiliation of Zebulun and Naphtali to purify the people of their sins, God has not abandoned us. God is with us. Let us maintain this great gift of faith! Let us pray and call upon our God! I am saddened to see so many pessimistic people who think that all is lost, that we are in a dead-end street. This cannot be! Perhaps we are living in the dark times of Zebulun and Naphtali, or we may feel like Isaiah, who did not experience the presence of Christ who came eight centuries later. We do not have to wait eight centuries, because Christ is present now in our history.

HOW CAN WE NOT BE FILLED with hope ourselves, sisters and brothers? In these days when we realize that our human strength can do no more, when we behold our homeland stuck in a dead-end alley, we realize that truly a transcendent salvation is needed. When we say, "Politics and diplomacy achieve nothing here; everything is destruction and disaster, and to deny it is madness," then truly a transcendent salvation is needed. Over these ruins of ours the glory of the Lord will shine. That is the great mission that Christians have at this critical moment of our land: keeping hope alive. We should not be expecting a utopia or entertaining illusions that drug us so that we can't see the reality. On the contrary, we should be closely observing this reality which by itself can yield nothing but which can still produce wonders if only we appeal to God's transcendent redemption.

Monday, March 10

I went to celebrate Mass in the presence of the bodies of nine people killed by the military repression, which have been in the cathedral since yesterday. . . . I used the message of the homily to say that those bodies are a lesson about the elevated destiny that human beings have – eternity. They are an indictment of the sin that rules on earth to such an extent that it can kill in this way. And I offered a word of encouragement for all of those who continue to struggle for the liberation of their people. . . .

In the afternoon Father Ramiro came to tell me that a very powerful bomb had been found in the basilica and that it could have gone off yesterday, possibly while we were celebrating the Mass at five o'clock for the eternal rest of Dr. Mario Zamora, at which there were many people. The bomb, which had been placed near the altar of St. Martha, was disarmed by police experts, who said it was strong enough to have destroyed the entire basilica and everyone who was there at the time. I thanked God, who has freed us from this new danger. . . . I also went with Father Ramiro to El Rosario Church to see the Dominican priests and to learn in more detail about the gunfire directed against it the night before.

8

Liberation

CHRIST PRESENTS HIMSELF to us with his great liberating work. I would like to explain this word "liberation" clearly. Many are fearful of this word; many also abuse this word. Well, there should be neither fear nor abuse. The truth is that "liberation" is a biblical word that expresses the whole work of the Lord in saving us from sin. The first liberation that Jesus proclaims is described marvelously by Saint Paul in Galatians 3: Christ has come to overthrow sin. By baptism, which cleanses us of sin, and by repentance, which converts us if we have grown apart from God, we are incorporated into Christ and become new men and new women. New human beings are the liberating work: it means making new men and new women who separate themselves from sin, cast aside their selfishness, idolatry, and pride and become humble followers of Christ the Lord.

"Because of faith in Jesus Christ, all are children of God" (Gal. 3:26). This is the work of Jesus: calling all people without discrimination. Saint Paul has stated

that there is no place for discrimination in Christianity:
"There does not exist among you Jew or Greek, slave
or freeman, male or female. All are one in Christ
Jesus" (Gal. 3:28). There are no longer social classes for
Christianity. There is no more racial discrimination. That
is why Christianity is shocking: because it must preach
this liberating work of declaring all men and women
equal in Christ Jesus. Interior renewal of the heart is
what makes all people equal, so let us renew ourselves!
As long as there are no new men and women, there will
only be pride and discrimination. Rich people and poor
people, when they are truly converted and interiorly
cleansed by this baptism of Christ, and when they truly
believe in the Lord, will no longer distinguish themselves
as rich or poor because there will be only a feeling of
fraternity in Christ Jesus. There is no longer superior and
inferior because both know that they are nothing in the
order of grace without Christ the Redeemer. Only one is
great: Christ who redeems us. There is only one liberator.

THE WORD "LIBERATION" BOTHERS many people,
but it is the reality of Christ's redemption. Liberation
does not mean only redemption after death, so that
people should just conform to the system while they
are alive. No, liberation is redemption that is already
beginning on this earth. Liberation means that the

exploitation of one human being by another no longer exists in the world. Liberation means redemption that seeks to free people from every form of slavery. Slavery is illiteracy; slavery is hunger, not having money to buy food; slavery is being homeless, not having a place to live. Slavery is misery; they go together. When the church preaches that Christ came to redeem us and that because of that redemption no form of slavery should exist on earth, the church is not preaching subversion or politics or communism. The church is preaching the true redemption of Christ. Christ does not want slaves; he wants all people to be redeemed; he wants us all, rich and poor, to love one another as sisters and brothers. He wants liberation to reach everywhere so that no slavery exists in the world, none at all. No person should be the slave of another, nor a slave of misery, nor a slave of anything that supposes sin in the world. This is the content of this revelation, this doctrine, this evangelization.

The church continues to preach that this kingdom of God proclaiming evangelization also wants to form community. As long as evangelization does not lead to a community, it is incomplete. When evangelization ends up forming a community, it means that I – as one who believes in Christ and his revelation, as one who believes in God and my temporal and eternal salvation – share this faith with other people who believe the same thing, and it means that we who believe the same thing form a community, a community of faith and love, a community of the redeemed. This is what the church is doing on earth: creating community. Therefore, when others try to scatter the communities, when terror is sown in those who proclaim the word of God and in those who meet to reflect on it, then there is persecution of the church. We have a right to meet together to complement one another and to help one another in our community reflection. In this way our faith keeps growing, our worship of God becomes more profound, and we become more united among ourselves. To create community is a command of Christ: "Go and proclaim the gospel to every creature. Gather together all those who share the same faith" (Mark 16:15). This is the church: the coming together of all those who believe in the one true God and in Christ the Redeemer.

DO NOT FEAR that those of us who speak about these issues have become communists or subversives. We are simply Christians who draw from the commands of the gospel the consequences that our people and all humankind need at this time. The gospel path leads that way: through poverty of spirit, through the struggle for justice, through the sowing of peace. The paths of the Beatitudes are today very dangerous paths, and that is why there are so few people willing to walk on them. Let us not be afraid! Let us keep walking on this road that will one day lead us to death so that people can pray for us, but so that we will also be saints in heaven participating in the glory of the risen Christ!

THE CHURCH CANNOT SEEK only liberation of a temporal nature. The church does not want to liberate poor people so that they can *have* more, but rather wants them to *be* more. She promotes people so that they *are* more. The church is hardly concerned with having more or having less. She is interested in making sure that all persons, whether they have many possessions or not, make progress and become true human beings and children of God. She wants people to be valued not for what they have but for what they are. This is the human dignity that the church preaches. It is the hope people have in their hearts that tells them: when you complete your life, you will participate in the kingdom of heaven. Don't expect a perfect paradise here, but the kingdom will exist to the extent that you work on this earth for a more just world, one in which you try to be more neighborly to your neighbors. This will also be your reward in eternity.

THE PROBLEM OF PEACE is immense, and it needs many peacemakers: priests, men and women religious, laity who are involved in every political and economic situation – the call goes out to all. The harvest is abundant. El Salvador possesses extraordinary vigor and exuberance. What a marvelous people El Salvador would be if Salvadorans were nurtured in an environment of peace, justice, love, and freedom! Let each one of us, according to our means, nurture this vocation to become instruments of peace. Jesus Christ in the Gospel and Saint Paul in his letter describe the conditions of those who want to be forgers of peace. We would do well to review this passage of the Gospel where Jesus preaches to us about the indispensable condition of being poor in spirit, of being detached: "Carry no money bag, no rucksack, no sandals – go as pilgrims" (Luke 10:4). This is the great adventure for us today. There are those who only seek security and comfort, who do not want to take the risk of poverty, who do not want to detach themselves from lucrative situations, not even in their hearts – these people do not want to collaborate with God.

But external poverty is not enough. I also want to address those who preach poverty and a church of the poor but do so insincerely, seeking demagogic praise – that does not help either. The poverty preached in today's Gospel is the poverty of Saint Paul: "I am crucified to the world" (Gal. 6:14). This is poverty that flows from love for Jesus Christ. It is poverty that beholds Christ naked on the cross and tells him, "I will follow you wherever you go, taking the roads of poverty, not out of demagogy but because I love you, because I want to be holy with my own holiness." This poverty makes me feel that the world's riches are crucified for me and that I am crucified by all the criteria of the world – this is true poverty.

Blessed are the poor of heart, those whose hearts feel the need for God, those who find the joy of life in the cross and sacrifice, those who have learned the true secret of peace in the crucified one. This secret consists of loving God to the extreme of letting oneself be killed for him and of loving one's neighbors to the point of being crucified for them. This is the love of the modern redeemers, the love of Christ, the love that endures forever. Only these will be the true peacemakers that Christ blessed in the Beatitudes: "Blessed are those who sow peace, for they will be called children of God" (Matt. 5:9). Let us promise this to the Lord while we proceed to proclaim our faith in him.

MANY PEOPLE WOULD LIKE poor people to keep on saying, "It is God's will that I live this way." But it is not the will of God that some people have everything while others have nothing. That cannot be of God. God's will is that all his children should be happy. When two or three agree in asking something of God, God grants it. That is the community of love, the will that unites in God. How marvelous it is to know that this morning also our prayer and our Mass will be heard by God because there are more than two of us! The cathedral is full, and so, united with Christ, we can ask the Father for what our society needs. Let us therefore make our Sunday Mass, as I said at the beginning, a time of hope.

THOSE WHO DO NOT PRAY because they kneel down before the god of materialism – be it money or politics or anything else – have not understood the true greatness of being a human person. To pray is to understand that this mystery of my existence as a man or a woman has limits, but precisely at those limits begins the infinite essence of the One with whom I am able to dialogue. . . .This is prayer, the ability of human beings to understand that they have been made by someone powerful, but that they have been elevated to be interlocutors with their Creator.

This is Pentecost; this is the church: bringing this message to humankind. That is why the church above all proclaims her religious mission and teaches people to pray. She is distressed when her children do not pray as we have so often urged. This is the soul of our church, sisters and brothers. The Holy Spirit is nothing more than that God who enters into communication with us and invites us to use our freedom and our intelligence in order to open ourselves to the Absolute and enter into dialogue with the One who created us, who made us capable of becoming his children, who awaits us in heaven, who consoles us on earth, and who leads us along paths that are worthy of the children of God.

THOSE WHO ARE TRULY HUMBLE do not hide their qualities. A humble person is one who says with Mary, "The mighty One has done great things for me" (Luke 1:49). Each one of us possesses greatness. God would not be my Author if I were something useless. I am worth a lot, you are worth a lot, we are all worth a lot because we are creatures of God, and God has poured out his gifts on each person.

That is why the church values human beings and fights for their rights, for their freedom, for their dignity. That is an authentic struggle of the church. As long as human rights are violated, as long as there are arbitrary arrests, as long as there are tortures, then the church considers herself persecuted as well. She feels distressed because she values human beings and cannot bear to see the image of God trampled upon by those who become brutish themselves by brutalizing others. The church wants to make that image of God more beautiful still, and so I tell you: however great your intellectual ability, your organizational skills, your willpower, your beauty, etc., there comes a moment when you realize that all of this will come to an end. At the moment you acknowledge your limitations, when you realize that there is something or someone beyond you, then you are already praying. You recognize that, as great as you may be, you are not God. There is a boundary beyond which you begin to feel the need for God. You need God and begin to pray, "Lord, help me in my limitations and in my smallness!" That is when I begin to see, in my limited greatness, the infinite greatness of God, and then begins my contemplation, my prayer, my petitions, my asking for pardon because I have offended God, and above all my giving of thanks: "Without you I am nothing."

WHEN WE DESPISE THE POOR PERSON or the harvester of coffee or sugar cane or cotton, it is the face of Christ we despise. Let us think of the campesinos who even today are traveling about in search of sustenance for the whole year. Let us not forget them, for they are the face of Christ. The face of Christ is there among the sacks and baskets of the harvesters. The face of Christ is there in the torture and cruelty of the prisons. The face of Christ is dying of hunger in the children who have nothing to eat. The face of Christ is the needy person who asks the church to speak out. How can the church refuse if it is Christ who is telling her, "Speak for me"? At the hour of that final judgment I don't want to be on the left side hearing the words: "Depart from me, you accursed, into the eternal fire, for I was hungry and you gave me no food. I was in need and you did not care for me" (Matt. 25:41–42). You were more concerned about the purity of your orthodoxy; you were more concerned about quiet time for your prayer; you were more concerned about your congregation or your school. You didn't want to contaminate yourself with derelicts. You were worried about your social and economic and political prestige, and that's why you despised those who were asking you for help – and there I was!" This is the norm by which Christ will judge us. His kingdom is love, a love that builds us up.

GOOD WORKS ARE the church's splendor. But notice how today's readings insist on good works for the sake of the poor. How beautiful and eloquent are Isaiah's words: "Share your bread with the hungry; shelter the homeless; clothe the naked when you see them, and do not turn your back on your own flesh" (Isa. 58:7). I am the one who is the beggar. It is my own flesh that is hungry, and so I provide food. The person who comes to me freezing and looking for shelter is my own flesh, and so I provide protection. Feel deeply this fraternity; feel deeply this identity. I don't mean just with yourself but above all with Christ. "Everything you do for that needy person, you do for me" (Matt. 25:40).

How can the church not be pained by a civilization of selfishness, this civilization of cruel inequalities where the poor, the helpless, the hungry, the naked, the homeless must exist as if they were not persons, were not our brothers and sisters! We have said before, sisters and brothers, that we are not defending laziness or idleness. Those who do not work, says the Bible, should not eat (2 Thess. 3:10). But we are dealing with situations that have become all too common among us, as if there were different classes of human beings: the rich and the poor. But we are all one and the same flesh! We have the same origin and the same destiny! Christ has loved all of us and identified with all of us!

Let us live doing good works. What does the prophet say? "When you do all this, then your light shall break forth like the dawn, and your wound shall be healed; your vindication shall go before you and the glory of the Lord shall be your rear guard" (Isa. 58:8). This is the glory that follows the church and those who live with justice and charity. That is why every one of us in this archdiocese must be enkindled with justice, freedom, equality, and defense of human rights, viewing them all in the light of the faith. . . .

"Then you shall call and the Lord will answer; you shall cry for help and he will say, 'Here I am!'" (Isa. 58:9). What more do we want than to enjoy God's nearness? The word of God today gives us one rule by which to judge whether God is near us or far away: God is near all those who are concerned for the hungry, the naked, the poor, the disappeared, the tortured, the imprisoned. All those who draw close to suffering flesh have God close at hand. "Cry for help, and he will hear you." Religion does not consist in a lot of praying. Religion consists in this guarantee of having God close to me because I lend a hand to my sisters and brothers.... Because that is where God is. The degree to which we approach the poor and how we approach them – whether with love or with scorn – determines how we approach God. What we do to the poor, we do also to God. The way we look at them is the way we look at God. God has so desired to be identified with them that the merits of each one of us and of our society will be measured by the way we treat the needy and the poor.

ANOTHER ROLE OF THE CHURCH is revealed in another Gospel passage: "Lord, teach us to pray." Jesus taught them to say "Father." This precious word would resolve everything. If we could only learn to call upon the Creator of all things as "Father," then we would feel that all of us are brothers and sisters, and we would pray, "Your kingdom come" (Luke 11:1–2). This is the deepest desire of the human heart because when God's kingdom comes on earth there will be more justice, more love, more harmony, and more equality among us all. Forgive us, for we are sinners. My sisters and brothers, this beautiful prayer is the height of human development. Human beings should be valued not for what they have but for what they are. And human beings most truly *are* when they come face to face with God and understand what marvels God has done with them. How God has created them as intelligent, free, and loving beings. . . .

Prayer also does not mean that you expect God to do what you can do. Do all that you can do. Put your technology to work; devise irrigation systems for your fields; fertilize your soil; feed your cattle as best you can. And after you have done all this, then pray. Don't expect everything from God, but after you have done everything you can, then leave the rest in God's hands. Do the same as those we mentioned here once before, those who prepared for a flight to the moon. A Christian technician said, "Technology has done everything that can be done. We hope this will be a success, but now all we can do is pray and ask God to bless our work." That is prayer, sisters and brothers. Prayer does not make us smaller. When we pray expecting God to do everything while we stand idle with our arms folded, then that is a false god. But when we work and develop our mind and our ability to organize, then we should say to God, "Lord, despite this mystery of greatness which I am, I understand that you are greater, that you embrace me, that you understand me, that you complete me...."

That is what the church is for: to teach people to pray. But the church must teach people to pray in the right way, not the lulling kind of prayer that says, "Resign yourself to living poorly, for after death God will give you heaven." This is not Christianity. That is why they accused us Christians of giving opium to the people. In this communism was right, because they were working hard while Christians were only praying and doing nothing. But Christianity proves to be better than communism when people work like communists and hope in God like Christians. Do you see the difference? The church must work for a twofold development, urging people to develop their abilities and bringing them to hope in the transcendent God without whom nothing is strong and nothing has value.

ISAIAH'S COMPARISON BECOMES even more poetic: "As the earth brings forth its plants and a garden makes its seeds spring up, so will the Lord make justice and praise spring up before all the nations" (Isa. 61:11).

I imagine that when a person sows a garden, she hopes
that flowers will sprout from the earth, but it is she
who has planted the seeds. This is what God has done
in redeeming us, as the prophet says, "He has sent me
to evangelize the poor, to announce the good news to
those who suffer, to bind up the hearts that are broken,
to proclaim amnesty for the captives and freedom for
the prisoners" (Isa. 61:1). Listen, is that not the voice of
the church here in El Salvador crying out, "Amnesty!
Freedom! No more torture! No more suffering!"? This
is the voice of God himself, who wants to sow goodness
and justice on earth so that this land will prosper. The
Lord has promised this, and he will not fail. When will
it come about? We don't know, but let us hope, like the
farmer who sows and is not impatient – in due course the
garden will flourish.

Sunday, March 16

This has been a day of great pastoral work and great satisfaction. The Mass at the basilica went on until ten-fifteen. I realize that I overdid the preaching, but the themes – the focus on a reality that is so dense – and the attention of the people encourage me not to neglect this opportunity to continue developing the Lenten catechesis, our thinking about the mystery of Christ that we are preparing for Holy Week, and also to give Christian guidelines for interpreting the very complex realities of our country.

Today I highlighted the repression, which has not ended but, instead, is getting worse. It is causing great pain and the Church must denounce it. . . .

Later we went to Aguilares where, at eleven-thirty, we celebrated Mass for the soul of Father Grande on the

third anniversary of his death. . . . I noticed the
absence of many of the people of Aguilares, for the
church was only half-filled and I could tell that the
majority of them were communities that had come from
elsewhere. This shows that the military repression in a
zone that has suffered so much is having the desired
effect of terrorizing the people and of distancing them
from those who can help them in their awareness and
in organization.

I used the opportunity to preach about this very
thing, using the Scripture reading that speaks to us
about Christ reconciling the world through his death
and his blood, of how the mystery of our church asks
us to sacrifice in the way that Father Grande was
asked, and for us to make an effort for the integral
liberation of our people without being afraid of
anything happening.

9

All Things New

THIS KING IS IMMORTAL, and his victory is
absolute. Saint Paul tells us that the principalities, the
powers, and the authorities will be destroyed and Christ's
enemies will be placed under his feet (1 Cor. 15:24–25).
This is a very picturesque way of portraying the destiny
of all the arrogance and bravado that is nowadays being
directed against the church. The persecution, the hatred,
and the defamation will come to naught, for God says,
"I will place your enemies as a footstool for your feet."
When all the powers have been dominated, Christ will
hand the kingdom over to the Father. He is the true
liberator who frees us from every form of servitude.
That's why when we proclaim here the kingdom of
Christ, we are not departing from our history. What
we are saying is that the plague of violence we are now
experiencing will also be subdued by God's kingdom and
those who are guilty of causing the violence will be made
footstools if they are not converted in time.

WHEN CHRIST SUMMONS the blessed ones, he speaks to them these words: "Come, blessed ones, and inherit the kingdom prepared for you from the creation of the world" (Matt. 25:34). This is not some improvised kingdom. Notice how history begins with God's will. While it is true that we humans participate actively in history, God is still the Lord of history, and all history flows from the will of God. Creation was God's first gesture. At first there was nothing existing, but then, when something began to exist, God already had his kingdom in mind. As the most noble members of this creation, human beings will arrive at the kingdom of salvation, the kingdom of glory. That's why the kingdom of Christ is eternal; it is not something invented by humans; it has its origin in God's mind. Christ is like a king who has brought all under his sway (1 Cor. 15:27). As he did on the cross, he speaks to his eternal Father those beautiful words that express the supreme satisfaction of one who has done his duty: *Consummatum est,* "It has been accomplished" (John 19:30). That's how I imagine Christ at the end of time: reigning as the universal king of all that has been won by his redemption, he declares, "Mission accomplished!"

Saint Paul says, "He will hand over his kingdom to the Father . . . so that God will be all in all" (1 Cor. 15:24–28). Can't you imagine what a glorious moment that will be when each of us creatures is even a tiny atom in that kingdom of creation that Christ will hand over to the Father, that kingdom that will never end? Who is ever left alone in history? What atom will become distant and lost? Everything is foreseen. Even the tiniest child, even the nameless campesino who harvests coffee, even the most insignificant person will find a place in this kingdom that Christ will hand over to the Father who will then be all in all without exception. Who will be great in the kingdom of heaven? Those who are most filled with Christ! . . .

When history ends and Christ hands history over to the Father, this kingdom will continue to exist eternally as an adornment, as a garment, as a palace, as a temple of God. We are, Saint Peter tells us, "living stones" building up that eternal kingdom of God (1 Pet. 2:5).

WE ARE IN THE FULLNESS OF TIME which stretches from the first coming of Christ and the origins of Christianity until the second coming. Saint Paul also refers to this fullness of time (Titus 2:13), telling us that even now there should be great joy among us as we celebrate the birth of Christ twenty centuries later, but there will be even greater joy when Christ returns to crown the fullness of time. Then he will gather together all the work of his church, all the good will of Christians, all

that has been sown in suffering and pain. We will all
be gathered together to become the definitive kingdom
that must come to fulfillment. That kingdom of justice
will come. That kingdom of peace will come. Let us
not be discouraged even when the horizon of history
appears dark and closed off, as if human realities made
it impossible for God's plans to be accomplished. God
can make use of human mistakes, even of people's sins,
to overcome the darkness, as Isaiah has said, so that
one day the people will sing not only of the return from
Babylon but of the complete liberation of humankind:
"The people who walked in darkness have seen a great
light; upon those who dwell in the land of gloom a light
has shone" (Isa. 9:1).

On this holy night, sisters and brothers, the light that
shines brilliantly in Bethlehem is a sign of our hope. Let
us not be discouraged when our hope is put to the test.
Let us hope against all hope and hold fast to this fullness of time. Let us live the ideal that God must make
real. Christmas is a message of optimism that I want to
engrave deeply in the heart of every Christian so that
tonight becomes, as the divine word tells us, a night that
marks the beginning of the kingdom of God that we
await with confidence.

AS LONG AS WE HAVE FAITH and hope in this
Christ who will return and in the realities that exist
beyond our own failures and our death and our difficulties, as long as we keep present that horizon, then
we are the Passover church, the church of hope. The
gospel speaks to us also about this eschatological sense:
"Foolish and slow to believe! Did he not have to suffer
all this so as to enter into glory?" (Luke 24:25–26).
Suffering is necessary, and we should not be surprised or
scandalized by afflictions and unexpected failures. . . .
Those who struggle for liberation and see their efforts
fail are tempted to say, "This is not solved with Christian
hope. We have to resort to violence." That is a lie. God
is patient because he is eternal. We must be patient with
him, awaiting the definitive heaven, the sure triumph,
the true Passover.

*On March 24, 1980, at six in the evening, Archbishop
Romero celebrated a memorial Mass for Sara Meardi de
Pinto, who had died the previous year. She was the mother
of a friend, Jorge Pinto, publisher and editor of one of the
few newspapers besides Romero's own* Orientación *to report
accurately on the government's crimes. That newspaper's
offices had been bombed three weeks before.*

DOÑA SARITA DEDICATED all her cultural formation and graciousness to the service of a cause that is
so necessary today: the true liberation of our people.
This afternoon, dear sisters and brothers, I believe we
should not only pray for the eternal rest of our dear
Sarita but should above all embrace this message that
every Christian today must heartily proclaim. Many
people don't understand the message. They think that
Christianity should not get involved in these things, but
quite the opposite is true. You just heard the Gospel of
Christ: we must not love our lives so much that we avoid
taking the risks in life that history calls for. Those who
seek to shun danger will lose their lives, whereas those
who for love of Christ dedicate themselves to the service
of others will live. They are like that grain of wheat
that dies, at least in appearance. If the grain does not
die, it remains alone (John 12:24–25). If it yields a crop,
it is because it dies, allowing itself to be immolated in
the earth; it is by being dismantled that it produces the
crop. . . .

This is the hope that inspires us as Christians. We
know that every effort to improve society, especially
when justice and sin are so widespread, is an effort
that God blesses, that God wants, that God requires of
us. . . . For we have the assurance that we will never fail

in all the work that we do on earth if we infuse it with Christian hope. We will find it purified in that kingdom where our merit will be according to what we have done on earth. . . .

I ask all of you, dear brothers and sisters, to view these things that are happening in our historical moment with a spirit of hope, generosity, and sacrifice. And let us do what we can. We can all do something and be more understanding. This holy woman whom we are remembering today perhaps could not do anything directly, but she encouraged those who were doing something, she understood their struggle, and she above all prayed. Even after death she speaks to us a message from eternity, telling us that our work is worthwhile. If we illuminate with Christian hope our intense longings for justice and peace and all that is good, then we can be sure that no one dies forever. If we have imbued our work with a sense of great faith, love of God, and hope for humanity, then all our endeavors will lead to the splendid crown that is the sure reward for the work of sowing truth, justice, love, and goodness on earth. Our work does not remain here; it is gathered and purified by the Spirit of God and returned to us as a reward.

This holy Mass of thanksgiving, then, is just such an act of faith. By Christian faith we know that at this moment the host of wheat becomes the body of the Lord who offered himself for the redemption of the world, and that the wine in this chalice is transformed into the blood that was the price of salvation. May this body that was immolated and this flesh that was sacrificed for humankind also nourish us so that we can give our bodies and our blood to suffering and pain, as Christ did, not for our own sake but to bring justice and peace to our people. Let us therefore join closely together in faith and hope at this moment of prayer for Doña Sarita and ourselves.

In that moment of prayer, a shot sounded in the chapel. Archbishop Romero fell to the floor at the foot of the cross behind the altar. He died within minutes.

TRUE LIBERATION is what Christ began to explain to the disciples of Emmaus: "'Was it not necessary,' he asked them, 'that the Messiah should suffer these things and so enter into his glory?' Then beginning with Moses and all the prophets, he interpreted to them what referred to him in all the scriptures" (Luke 24:26–27). The redemption and the liberation that the church preaches and longs for is not a liberation that disappoints even when things turn out badly, even when people must die on a cross, even when people are tortured and killed because of the cruelty of those who do not want to hear cries of true liberation. These are episodes in Christ's war to save the world. Let us not forget, sisters and brothers, that redemption is still taking place.

Notes

Introduction: Who Was Oscar Romero?

3 *Peace is not found* Bishops of Latin America, *Peace,* The Medellin Documents, Second General Conference of Latin American Bishops, Medellin, Colombia, September 6, 1968.

7 *We have asked* Oscar Romero, *A Prophetic Bishop Speaks to his People: The Complete Homilies of Archbishop Oscar Arnulfo Romero*, vol. 1. Translated by Joseph Owens, SJ (Miami: Convivium Press, 2015, 2017), 62.

10 *We have never* Ibid., vol. 2, 53.

11 *I want to reaffirm* Ibid., vol. 4, 190.

13 *I express my consecration* Irene B. Hodgson, *Archbishop Oscar Romero: A Shepherd's Diary* (Cincinnati: St. Anthony Messenger Press, 1993), 11.

You can tell them Michael J. Walsh, *Voice of the Voiceless* (Maryknoll, NY: Orbis Books, 1985), 50–51.

Brothers, you are a part Kevin Clarke, *Oscar Romero: Love Must Win Out* (Collegeville, MN: Liturgical Press, 2014), 21.

1 The Creator

16 *A visit to the town* April 8, 1978; *A Shepherd's Diary,* 31

18 *How wonderful it is* July 23, 1978; *A Prophetic Bishop Speaks to his People* vol. 3, 115–16

19 *The Bible says* July 23, 1978; vol. 3, 115–16

Only when we see May 21, 1978; vol. 2, 461

20 *There is no anonymous person* June 24, 1979; vol. 5, 53

21 *The whole history of Israel* March 16, 1980; vol. 6, 366–368

22 *Let us look this morning* January 8, 1978; vol. 2, 188

Notes

2 The Word Made Flesh

24 *In the afternoon*   October 9, 1978; *Diary,* 86

26 *Christ is being born for us*   December 24, 1978; vol. 4, 120–21

  God so loved the world   May 21, 1978; vol. 2, 459

27 *If we want to find*   December 24, 1979; vol. 6, 116–117

28 *Mary knew how to endure*   December 24, 1979; vol. 6, 117–118

29 *Saint Paul told the Corinthians*   February 18, 1979; vol. 4, 217–18

30 *As we behold the risen Christ*   March 26, 1978; vol. 2, 332–33

32 *He is Messiah and Lord*   April 16, 1978; vol. 2, 382–83

  The prophecy of Isaiah   January 14, 1979; vol. 4, 171–72

33 *As long as we do not see*   March 26, 1978; vol. 2, 332–33

35 *Christians must always nourish*   May 20, 1979; vol. 4, 427–28

3 Redemption

36 *In the evening*   April 2, 1978; *Diary,* 21

38 *Christ incarnates the whole history*   March 23, 1978; vol. 2, 314–15

39 *The Servant of God is like*   March 24, 1978; vol. 2, 320

41 *Yes, in Christ is revealed*   December 25, 1977; vol. 2, 145–46

  In Matthew, Chapter 20   September 24, 1978; vol. 3, 258–60

44 *The redemption planned by God*   December 18, 1977; vol. 2, 121–22

45 *This is a night of triumph*   March 25, 1978; vol. 2, 329

46 *As long as Christ had not risen*   April 15, 1979; vol. 4, 370–71

4 The Call

48 *Bishop Rivera also came*   May 18, 1979; *Diary,* 229

49 *Tonight Father Gregorio Rosa*   May 21, 1979; *Diary,* 233

50 *The risen Christ must now*   November 27, 1977; vol. 2, 54–55

  The magi asked   January 6, 1980; vol. 6, 155

78 *Christ tells us*   April 30, 1978; vol. 2, 411

79 *Saint Paul tells*   December 17, 1978; vol. 4, 87, 89

81 *What did that Spirit*   April 22, 1979; vol. 4, 388

82 *It is our own church community*   December 17, 1978; vol. 4, 86–87

83 *God wants to save us*   January 15, 1978; vol. 2, 201

   The vocation of human beings   July 23, 1978; vol. 3, 123

84 *Paul then went*   October 29, 1978; vol. 3, 327

86 *If you want to hear*   January 27, 1980; vol. 6, 225–226

87 *How much goodness*   October 8, 1978; vol. 3, 292

88 *The day when we understand*   November 6, 1977; vol. 1, 412–13

   The church has inspired   August 6, 1977; vol. 1, 236–37

7   The Kingdom

90 *I went to Domus Mariae*   February 14, 1980; *Diary,* 488

92 *Isaiah presents us with*   October 23, 1977; vol. 1, 386

   Christ is already building   December 24, 1977; vol. 2, 136–37

93 *The church is not*   July 30, 1978; vol. 3, 132

94 *There is no longer distinction*   January 8, 1978; vol. 2, 189

95 *When the wise men came*   December 25, 1977; vol. 2, 150

95 *There must have been*   July 9, 1978; vol. 3, 94

97 *With the coming of Christ*   December 24, 1977; vol. 2, 135

   The light of God   January 8, 1978; vol. 2, 192

98 *This year is ending*   December 31, 1977; vol. 2, 160–61

99 *Isaiah announced*   August 21, 1977; vol. 1, 265

100 *If we are reasonable*   August 7, 1977; vol. 1, 245

101 *The prophet Isaiah says*   January 22, 1978; vol. 2, 212–13

102 *How can we not be filled*   January 7, 1979; vol. 4, 149–150

8 Liberation

9 All Things New

Bibliography

Brockman, James R. *Romero: A Life.* Maryknoll, NY: Orbis Books, 1989.

Clarke, Kevin. *Oscar Romero: Love Must Win Out.* Collegeville, MN: Liturgical Press, 2014.

Romero, Oscar. *A Prophetic Bishop Speaks to His People: The Complete Homilies of Archbishop Oscar Arnulfo Romero,* 6 vols. Translated by Joseph Owens, SJ. Miami: Convivium Press, 2015, 2017.

_____ . *A Shepherd's Diary.* Translated by Irene B. Hodgson. Cincinnati: St. Anthony Messenger Press, 1993.

_____ . *The Violence of Love.* Compiled and translated by James R. Brockman, SJ. Maryknoll, NY: Orbis Books, 2004.

Walsh, Michael J. *Voice of the Voiceless.* Maryknoll, NY: Orbis Books, 1985.

Plough Spiritual Guides

The Reckless Way of Love
Notes on Following Jesus
Dorothy Day

Love in the Void
Where God Finds Us
Simone Weil

The Prayer God Answers
Eberhard Arnold and Richard J. Foster

Why We Live in Community
Eberhard Arnold and Thomas Merton

The Two Ways
The Early Christian Vision of Discipleship
from the Shepherd of Hermas and the Didache
Introduction by Rowan Williams

Plough Publishing House
845-572-3455 ◆ info@plough.com
PO BOX 398, Walden, NY 12586, USA
Robertsbridge, East Sussex TN32 5DR, UK
4188 Gwydir Highway, Elsmore, NSW 2360, Australia
www.plough.com

Want to give this book to a friend? And keep it too? Now you can:
if you pass this book on, we're happy to replace it for free.
For details visit plough.com/give.